Cordon Bleu

Fish 1

Cordon Bleu

Fish 1

CBC / B.P.C. Publishing Ltd.

Published by
B.P.C. Publishing Ltd.,
P.O. Box 20,
Abingdon, Oxon.

Designed by Melvyn Kyte
Printed and bound in England
by Waterlow (Dunstable) Limited

These recipes have been adapted from the Cordon Bleu Cookery Course
published by Purnell in association with the London Cordon Bleu
Cookery School
Principal : Rosemary Hume ; Co-Principal : Muriel Downes

Contents

Introduction

Round fish, flat fish, shellfish, white fleshed fish, oily fish — the waters of the world are full of a variety of fish that provides one of the greatest natural sources of food, apparently still flourishing and almost never cultivated. The coasts of the British Isles have their fair share, and the inland waters make their contribution too. Yet considering that Britain is a smallish island, and nowhere is more than half a day's journey from the sea, we eat surprisingly little fish.

People who live on the coasts naturally make good use of the food supply on their doorsteps. For the rest of us, it is presumably a hang-over from the days when transport was not up to carrying fish inland fast enough that holds us back. But in days when meat prices rise constantly, fish could well play a larger part in our household budgeting. Rich in protein, scarcely less so than meat, fish should be part of the staple diet of any family. And with a Cordon Bleu recipe selected from this book, we think you will please any lovor of good food.

When you go out to buy fish, don't decide which type you want until you have seen what the fishmonger is offering — availability and prices vary tremendously almost from day to day as the shoals move in and out of our fishing waters. The most important factor Is freshness — firm, wet-looking fish with plenty of scales or natural slime and bright, protruding eyes are what you are looking for. If the eyes have sunk into the head or if the fish is soft and limp when lifted from the slab — leave it there.

This is a book of fairly simple fish recipes. We have started by setting out the basic methods of cooking fish plainly, and then selected some of our favourite recipes that even beginners can try. At the end is an appendix containing notes on various items that recur throughout the book, and a glossary of some of the less familiar cooking terms that we use.

With this book beside you, we hope you can do justice to any fish on the market. Later in the series we are going to collect together some more advanced fish recipes for you to try your hand at. For experienced cooks, we have included lots of information about the fish themselves, and we hope there will be some new recipes for you to try — even the simplest can grace a dinner party if well prepared by an enthustiastic Cordon Bleu cook.

Rosemary Hume
Muriel Downes

Ways of cooking fish

Whether you choose a rich, oily fish such as herring or salmon, or a milder, finer fleshed white fish, or a gourmet's shellfish, there are dozens of ways to cook it. Plainly grilled or fried and served with lemon and a light garnish are sure winners ; or you can try it boiled, steamed or poached and served in a rich creamy sauce.

For an easily digestible meal for an invalid, serve white fish without a sauce. Or if you feel really adventurous, for a party serve a classic fish and pastry dish, salmon tourtière.

Preparation

To clean round fish

Rinse in cold water, then scrape with the back of a knife from tail to head to remove scales; this applies particularly to scaly fish, such as herrings and salmon.

For large round fish, such as haddock, codling, sea trout, take a sharp knife and slit the skin from just below the head, along belly to the vent. Scrape out the gut and discard it; the head may then be cut off. Hold fish under a running cold tap to clean it thoroughly. If there is any black skin inside the cavity (sometimes there is, even though the fish has been bought gutted), gently rub it away with a damp cloth dipped in salt.

To skin large fillets of round fish

Lay the fillet skin side down on the board, lift the tail end and slip a thin, sharp knife between the flesh and skin. Dip the fingers of your left hand in salt to prevent slipping and, holding the tail skin firmly, saw the flesh away from the skin, keeping the knife at an angle to the board (see diagram 1).

To clean flat fish

With fish such as plaice or sole, make a semi-circular cut just below the head on the dark side, scrape out the gut and wash fish thoroughly.

To skin flat fish

Sole may be skinned whole and the fishmonger will skin them on both sides if asked.

When doing it yourself, trim away the outside fins with scissors. Lay the fish on the board and, starting at the head end, slip your thumb about 1 inch under the black skin at the cut where the fish was cleaned (diagram 2). Run your thumb right round the fish, then grasp the tail end of the skin firmly and rip it off (diagram 3). Repeat this on the other side of the fish.

Plaice are skinned after filleting, as the skin is thick and would tear the flesh if ripped off. Skin as for large fillets.

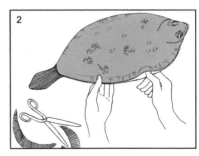

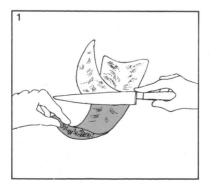

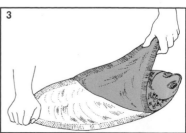

To fillet round fish

Lay the fish on a piece of wet, rough cloth, or sacking (to prevent slipping) and keep fish steady with one hand. Take a thin sharp knife or filleting knife, and first trim away the fins then cut down the back with the blade on top of the backbone (see diagram 4). Lift off the top fillet. Now slip the knife under the bone at the head, and keeping it as close as possible to the back bone, work down to the tail, using short sharp strokes, at the same time keeping a firm hold on the head end with the other hand (see diagram 5).

To fillet flat fish

Plaice and sole (if weighing no more than 1-1½ lb) are usually cut into a double fillet. This means that the flesh on both sides of the backbone, top and underside, is taken off in one piece, ie. two fillets only for each fish. These may be divided into two for cooking. Lemon sole is treated in the same way.

If filleting at home, it is easier to take the flesh off in four fillets. Run the point of the knife down the backbone and with short, sharp strokes keeping the knife on the bone, work from the head outwards until the tail is reached and the fillet is detached (see diagram 6). Turn the fish round and starting from the tail take the other half of the fillet off in the same way (see diagram 7). Then turn the fish over and repeat the process. Flat fish fillets are larger and thicker on the dark side, which is uppermost when the fish is swimming.

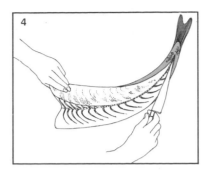

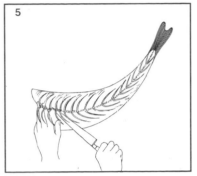

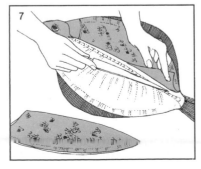

Grilling

Grilling is a good and attractive way of cooking small whole fish (round or flat), particularly the rich and oily varieties such as herring and mackerel. The intense heat crisps the skin, making the fish especially appetising. Sole, halibut, turbot and salmon steaks are excellent as straightforward grills.

Fish should not be salted before grilling but served with a savoury butter, such as maître d'hôtel, anchovy or orange, which gives all the seasoning necessary ; watercress makes a good garnish.

Unlike oily fish, white fish needs to be well brushed, both before and during cooking, with melted butter, or for a better colour clarified butter.

When grilling round fish score, ie. make a diagonal cut to slit the skin, in 2 or 3 places to allow the heat to penetrate more easily and so shorten the cooking time. It is not necessary to score flat fish unless they are very large. Grilling time depends on the thickness of the fish, not on the weight.

Mackerel
These are larger than herrings and a big one can weigh over a pound. They are excellent grilled whole or filleted. Score fish 3 times on each side. Brush with oil or melted butter. Grill whole fish for 10-15 minutes, filleted fish for 8 minutes on the cut side and 3-4 on the skin side.

Serve with maître d'hôtel butter and / or quarters, or slices, of lemon.

Herring
Grill these whole, or split open (in which case the backbone and many of the side bones may be removed). If grilling whole, cut off the heads and score herring twice on each side. Brush with oil or melted butter, then grill for 4-5 minutes on each side, 8-10 minutes in all.

For split or filleted herring, brush with butter and grill on cut side first for 5-6 minutes, then turn and allow a further 2-3 minutes on the skin side.

Dish up and serve piping hot with maître d'hôtel or mustard butter.

Sole and plaice
The best type for grilling is black or Dover sole. These may be in the form of small slip soles (8-10 oz each), or larger, one of which is sufficient for 2 people.

Ask your fishmonger to skin the sole on both sides. Grill with the head on, first brushing well with melted or clarified butter. Brush again from time to time and turn after 5-6 minutes. When nicely brown, dish up and pour over any juices from the grill pan.

Put a pat or two of maître d'hôtel butter on each sole before serving.

Treat plaice in the same way but fillet before skinning. Serve as for sole.

Salmon steaks
(4-6 oz steak per person)
While grilling salmon steaks keep them succulent by brushing frequently with melted or clarified butter.

Serve with maître d'hôtel or orange butter.

Halibut or turbot steaks

(6 oz steak per person)

Of all the white fish, with the exception of sole, these are best for grilling as they are firm-fleshed and less likely to break up when being turned.

For a good even colour, first dip in a little milk and then roll in seasoned flour before brushing with melted, or clarified, butter. The steaks must be kept well brushed and basted with the butter while grilling. Allow 8-10 minutes in all for steaks $\frac{3}{4}$-1 inch thick, turning once.

Dish up and top each with a pat of savoury butter (maître d'hôtel, anchovy or orange).

To 'vandyke' the tail of a fish, accentuate the line by cutting an acute V-shape and making two distinct points. This is aptly named after the style of small, pointed beard made famous by Anthony Van Dyck, the 17th-century Court painter to Charles I.

Grilled mackerel are served here with lemon and boiled potatoes

Frying

There are two ways of frying fish, either in shallow or deep fat. It is important to know how to prepare fish for frying, and on pages 16 and 17 we give the different coatings, with step-by-step photographs of how to egg and crumb.

Fried fish should look appetising and taste light, leaving you wanting more.

Shallow fat frying

This is the most commonly used method and, as the name implies, it is done in a frying pan, in any of these fats : butter ; oil ; a mixture of butter and oil ; dripping ; lard or one of the commercially prepared fats.

Small whole fish, fillets of fish and fish cakes are suited to shallow fat frying. For the best taste and effect use butter, otherwise oil or dripping (do not use the latter with fish in an egg and crumb coating because dripping would over-brown the egg).

The amount of fat in the pan is important ; it should come half way up the fish so that the sides are completely browned.

Turn the fish once only and cook on moderate to brisk heat.

The same pan can be used for all types of food fried in shallow fat, any fat left over being strained off and used again, but fish fat should be kept only for fish frying.

Whole fish need only to be rolled in seasoned flour or oatmeal just before frying. Sole or plaice fillets may be rolled in seasoned flour and then fried in butter, or dipped in beaten egg after being rolled in seasoned flour, then fried until golden-brown.

1 *Coating skinned fillets of sole with seasoned flour for shallow frying*
2 *Lowering the floured fillets, skin side uppermost, into foaming butter*

14

Deep fat frying

This method is quicker than shallow fat frying as food is immersed completely. Therefore the fish needs a coating to protect it from the great heat of the fat.

When cool, strain used fat through muslin into a bowl, cover when it is quite cold, and store in a cool place until needed again.

Choose a deep, heavy gauge pan (fat bath or deep fryer) which covers the source of heat, complete with a wire basket to fit. Or buy a separate folding wire basket for fitting into any saucepan (which must, however, be of reasonably heavy gauge because fat is heated to high temperatures in deep fat frying). This separate basket is useful because its flexibility means it can also be used in an ordinary frying pan for cooking small foods such as croûtons.

When frying fish coated in soft batter mixture, you may find it easier to fry them in a fat bath without using a wire basket since batter tends to stick to the basket.

Suitable fats to use are : vegetable or nut oil ; lard ; clarified dripping or commercially prepared fat, but it is better not to mix these. Olive oil and margarine are not suitable for deep frying. The pan should not be more than one-third full of fat or oil.

Melt the fat, or put the oil, over moderate heat, then increase heat until right cooking temperature is reached (350-375°F). Oil must never be heated above 375°F and for sunflower oil, and some commercially prepared fats (eg. Spry, Cookeen), 360°F is the highest recommended temperature. It is important to remember that oil does not 'haze', as solid fats do, until heated to a much higher temperature than is required — or is safe — for frying.

The fat or oil should never be below 340°F, as it is essential that the surface of the food is sealed immediately. This means that it does not absorb the fat, and is more digestible.

The best way of testing temperature is with a frying thermometer. Before using, it should be stood in a pan of hot water then carefully dried before putting into the fat bath. The hot water warms the glass so that it does not break when plunged into the hot fat.

If you have no thermometer, drop in a small piece of food (eg. a chip). If the fat or oil is at the right temperature, the food will rise immediately to the top and bubbles appear round it. Alternatively drop in a cube of day-old bread, which should turn golden-brown in 20 seconds at 375°F ; 60 seconds at 360°F.

How to fry fish

For fish such as fillets of sole, or plaice, or small whole sole, an egg and breadcrumb coating is best.

Fish, such as haddock or whiting, which crumble more easily, are best fried in batter.

Most fried fish should be garnished with sprays of fried parsley and a savoury butter such as maître d'hôtel or anchovy, which should be served separately.

Watchpoint Great care should be taken when handling a deep

15

Frying continued

fat bath or fryer. When fat is heating, make sure that the handle of the fat bath or fryer is pushed to one side so that there is no danger of it being caught or knocked over.

Fat is inflammable ; if any is spilt, wipe it up at once. Keep the outside of the fat bath clean so that there is no chance of any fat catching alight, which can easily happen if it is overheated.

If fat does catch fire, smother it with a cloth — do not splash water on it or attempt to move the blazing pan. If you have to leave the kitchen at any time while cooking with fat, turn off the heat under the pan.

Fritter batter

10 oz plain flour
pinch of salt
1 oz fresh yeast, or 2 teaspoons
  dried yeast
2 teacups warm water
2 tablespoons oil
2 egg whites (optional)

Method
Sift flour and salt into a warm basin. Mix yeast in about half the warm water, stir into flour with oil. Add rest of water to make consistency of thick cream. Beat well and cover, leave in a warm place for 15-20 minutes, by then mixture should be well risen. If using egg white, whisk stiffly and fold into batter just before frying.

Fish in batter

For white fish such as haddock or cod fillet, allow $1\frac{1}{4}$-$1\frac{1}{2}$ lb for 4 people ; skin fish and cut into 4 oz portions. Sprinkle lightly with salt and lemon juice, and leave for 30 minutes. Drain off any liquid, dry well and roll in seasoned flour.

Have batter ready in a bowl before heating fat. When fat is hot, drop a piece of the fish into the batter bowl, turn to coat thoroughly, then lift out with a draining spoon and slide carefully into the fat bath. Fry about three pieces at a time, allowing plenty of room to turn them. When well browned and crisp, lift out and drain well on absorbent paper. Take out any scraps of batter before frying the next batch.

Egging and crumbing

To make egging and crumbing easy, it is best to follow a certain technique. Whether frying fish or shaping a mixture, the first coating should always be of flour, lightly seasoned with a pinch of salt and half as much pepper.

Start with a board or plate well sprinkled with seasoned flour on the one side, have the beaten egg on a plate in the centre, and the white crumbs on a large piece of paper on the other side. You can then work from left to right, or vice versa, finally placing the coated food on to a large dish.

If using a mixture, first divide this into even-size portions, then shape on the floured board or plate (preferably with palette knives or round-bladed knives to avoid touching with your fingers). With the knives, lift the shaped mixture into the beaten egg (brushing evenly) and on to the paper of crumbs,

1 *Divide mixture into even-size portions, shape on floured board*
2 *Lift the shaped mixtures with palette knives into beaten egg*

3 *Brush shapes evenly and then turn with the palette knives*
4 *After tipping in the paper of crumbs, press on with knives*

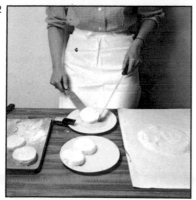

still not touching with your fingers. Lift each corner of the paper, tipping mixture from side to side, and when well covered, press on the crumbs with a knife. Then lift off on to the large dish already sprinkled with crumbs. The croquettes — the name given to this type of crumbed mixture — are then ready for frying.

In the case of fillets of fish, these must be absolutely dry, so make sure that after washing they are thoroughly dried in absorbent paper or a cloth kept specially for this purpose.

Roll fillets in the seasoned flour and shake gently to remove any surplus. Then draw them through the beaten egg, first on one side, then the other, and gently run down the whole length of the fillet with your finger and thumb to wipe off any surplus egg. Turn on to the paper of crumbs, tip fillets from side to side to cover thoroughly and press on the crumbs with a palette knife until well coated. Lift off on to a dish or rack. When convenient, egging and crumbing may be done quite a time ahead.

Fish cakes

This is a good way of using up leftovers. Make with white fish, fresh or canned salmon. The proportion of fish when cooked, skinned and flaked, should be equal that of potato. However, the fish can be more in quantity but never less.

1 lb fresh haddock, or cod fillet,
　or 12 oz cooked fish
little salt ⎫
butter 　⎬ if using fresh fish
lemon juice ⎭ 　only
3-4 medium-size potatoes
1 tablespoon butter
1 egg
salt and pepper
1 dessertspoon chopped parsley

For frying
seasoned flour
beaten egg
dry white crumbs

Method
With fresh fish, wash and dry well, sprinkle with a little salt and, if time allows, let it stand for 15-20 minutes. Tip off liquid, place fish in buttered, fireproof dish, with a little lemon juice, cover with buttered paper and cook for 15-20 minutes in the oven at 350°F or Mark 4. Flake fish, remove skin and bones.

Now work prepared fish in a bowl to break up the fibres (if fish is inclined to be wet, eg. cold or canned salmon, this working of fish will thicken the consistency.)

Boil potatoes, drain, dry and mash well. Beat in the butter, egg and fish ; season well and add parsley. Put out in tablespoons on to a seasoned, floured board. Shape into cakes, brush with beaten egg, roll in (and press on) the crumbs. Fry in either deep or shallow fat, when fat should be over $\frac{1}{2}$ inch deep in pan. Lift in the fish cakes when the fat is at the right temperature (350-375°F) and after browning on one side turn carefully. Drain when a good colour and serve hot with a tomato sauce or ketchup.

or tray. Leave for 1-2 minutes before lifting out fillets on to a hot dish. Scatter over fried parsley and serve pats of maître d'hôtel butter separately.

Lowering twisted fillet into fat

Fried fillets of sole or plaice

As a main course, allow 2 fillets per person from a fish weighing about $1\frac{1}{4}$ lb (skinned on both sides). Wash the fillets, dry thoroughly and roll in seasoned flour, beaten egg and white crumbs.

When ready to fry, heat the fat bath and place the basket in it. When the correct temperature is reached, take up fillets, hold each end between a finger and thumb and twist them. (This is done to avoid sogginess when deep fat frying. It reduces the flat surface which would normally come in too much contact with the serving dish and the other fillets. The resulting fillets also look more attractive.

Lower the twisted fillets to the surface of the fat and gently let go ; put in about three at a time. When fillets are a deep golden-brown, lift out the basket and stand it on a plate

Baking

This method is used for whole stuffed fish or cutlets. They should be basted frequently throughout cooking with hot fat or oil, or sometimes a marinade. Some fish, eg. mackerel and red mullet, can be baked 'en papillote' ie. completely enclosed in buttered greaseproof paper or foil, in which case basting is not necessary.

Poaching

Poaching is cooking in a small quantity of liquid in the oven, or on top of the cooker at a temperature which does not exceed 190°F. The resulting juices can then be used in a sauce.

Fish cooked in this way, whether whole or as a large steak, is nicest done in a special stock — court bouillon — rather than water. This is simple to prepare, and once the fish has been cooked in it, the liquid should be strained off and used again for poaching, or for a sauce. Larger pieces of fish are usually put into a tepid court bouillon, which gives a better colour to the fish, but with smaller cutlets you should use a hot one which prevents too much seepage from the fish. Fish cooked in a fair amount of liquid should be tied in muslin first.

If the fish is to be coated with sauce, it should first be transferred into a clean serving dish. If the sauce is served separately, it is traditional to serve the fish in a napkin, so no liquid is visible.

Cooking times

Large whole fish up to 6 lb : allow 8-10 minutes to the lb.
Fillets : 8-12 minutes.
Steaks or cutlets : 10-20 minutes according to thickness. The fish is cooked when the bone can easily be detached from the flesh.

Small whole fish : (eg. sole, whiting or plaice) : 15-20 minutes.

Au gratin

This is a less well-known method, in which small whole fish, fillets or steaks, are cooked in the oven in a thick, well-seasoned sauce and finished with a topping of browned breadcrumbs, melted butter and sometimes cheese (see cod au gratin, page 24).

Steaming

Fillets or cutlets of fish are placed on a buttered plate, seasoned lightly, covered with a little milk, a pat of butter, greaseproof paper and topped by a second plate, and cooked over a pan of gently simmering water. It is a method very suitable for invalids.

Court bouillon

(2 pint quantity)

2 pints water
1 carrot (sliced)
1 onion (stuck with a clove)
bouquet garni
6 peppercorns
2 tablespoons vinegar
salt

Method
Place all ingredients in a pan, salt lightly and bring to boil. Cover the pan with a lid and simmer for 15-20 minutes. Strain before using.

White fish

Delicate flavoured white fish are amongst the most prized dishes at a gourmet's table. Lean and easily digestible, they lend themselves to almost every form of preparation.
Try a Dover sole as a luxury, or show your culinary prowess by turning one of the humbler white fish into a tempting party dish.
With plainer home cooking in mind, poached or steamed white fish are ideal for children or invalids.

1 Haddock. 2 Skate. 3 Herring. 4 Plaice. 5 Lemon Sole. 6 Red mullet. 7 Grey mullet.

23

Cod

In season all the year round, this deep-sea fish can weigh from $1\frac{1}{4}$-20 lb. It is at its best from May to October. To serve this creamy flaked fish well you should first wash and dry it, rub the skin with a freshly cut lemon and then lightly sprinkle it with salt. After leaving for 30-60 minutes in a cool place, tip away any liquid and wipe the fish again.

Cod au gratin

$1\frac{1}{2}$ lb cod fillet, or frozen cod steaks
salt and pepper
1 tablespoon grated cheese
1 tablespoon browned crumbs
1 tablespoon melted butter

For béchamel sauce
$\frac{1}{2}$ pint milk
1 slice of onion
$\frac{1}{2}$ bayleaf
1 blade of mace
6 peppercorns
1 oz butter
1 oz plain flour

To save time in the preparation and cooking we would serve frozen spinach, either leaf or purée, with this dish. Creamed potatoes could be cooked and completed in the time it takes to bake the fish.

Method
Skin, wash and dry the fillet and place it on a plate. If using frozen cod steaks, allow them to thaw slowly. Dust cod lightly with salt and leave for 30 minutes.

To prepare béchamel sauce : scald the milk in a pan with the onion, bayleaf, mace and peppercorns, infuse for 10 minutes, then strain and reserve.

Melt the butter, draw pan aside and blend in the flour and flavoured milk ; season with salt, stir over gentle heat until boiling, then simmer for 2-3 minutes. Taste for seasoning. Tip sauce into a basin, cover with buttered paper to prevent a skin forming leave to cool. Set oven at 375°F or Mark 5.

Tip away any liquid that has run from the fish, pat it dry with absorbent paper, then cut in even-size pieces ; put these into a buttered ovenproof dish. Spoon the cold sauce over the fish and dust with the cheese and crumbs mixed together ; sprinkle with the melted butter and bake in pre-set oven for 25-30 minutes.

Watchpoint It is important that the fish should cover the bottom of the dish, then any cooking juices will blend with the white sauce. The brown crumbs mixed with the cheese give fish a good crisp coating when baked and prevent any 'pools' of fat forming on the top, which might happen if cheese only were used.

Cod cutlets bretonne

4 large cod steaks (1-inch thick)
squeeze of lemon juice
¼ pint dry cider
salt and pepper
5 tablespoons water
1 medium-size carrot
1 medium-size onion
2 sticks of celery
1 oz butter
1 tablespoon plain flour
2-3 tablespoons creamy milk
1 dessertspoon chopped parsley

Portions of haddock fillet are also suitable for cooking in this way.

Cod cutlets bretonne are poached in cider, then served in a creamy sauce with a garnish of vegetables

Method

Wash fish and dry in absorbent paper. Sprinkle lightly with lemon juice and salt and leave for 30 minutes. Dab away any liquid before lifting into a buttered ovenproof dish. Set oven at 350°F or Mark 4.

Pour over half the cider and add water. Cover with buttered paper and poach for 10-15 minutes in the pre-set oven.

Cut prepared vegetables into thin shreds and put into a small pan with a nut of the butter and 1 tablespoon of remaining cider. Cover tightly, cook 2-3 minutes, then put in oven to finish cooking. Take up fish, carefully pull out centre bone and peel off skin ; lift each piece on to a hot serving dish.

When vegetables are cooked, spoon them over the fish and keep warm. Strain fish liquid into the pan, add rest of cider, boil for 2-3 minutes to reduce, then draw aside. Work rest of butter and the flour to a paste (kneaded butter) and add it to liquid in 2-3 pieces. When dissolved, return to heat and stir until boiling, adjust seasoning and add milk and parsley. The sauce should be the consistency of cream ; add more kneaded butter to thicken if necessary. Spoon sauce over fish and serve very hot. Served with creamed potatoes this makes a good main dish.

Cod boulangère (cooked in butter with onions and potatoes)

1½ lb steak of cod
2-3 oz butter
3-4 medium-size potatoes
½ lb button onions
1 teaspoon granulated sugar (for dusting)
squeeze of lemon juice
chopped parsley

Method

Set the oven at 350°F or Mark 4. Wash and dry cod. Bone steaks and cut into large chunks. Place on an ovenproof dish, melt half the butter and pour over the fish. Cook in the pre-set oven for about 15 minutes, basting occasionally.

Quarter the potatoes length-ways and trim off the sharp edges. Blanch and drain. Turn them into a frying pan and sauté gently in half the remaining butter until golden-brown. Take out and set aside.

Blanch and drain the onions and fry in the same way in the rest of the butter, adding a dusting of sugar. Cover pan when onions are brown and continue to cook for a few minutes until just tender.

Baste fish once more and surround with the onions and potatoes. Cook in the oven for a further 5 minutes. Squeeze over a little lemon juice and sprinkle well with chopped parsley.

Finished cod boulangère with sauté potatoes and onions

Poached cod with egg or oyster sauce

2 lb steak of cod (or turbot, or halibut)

For court bouillon
2 pints water
1 large carrot (sliced)
1 onion (sliced)
bouquet garni
6 peppercorns
2 tablespoons vinegar, or juice of
$\frac{1}{2}$ lemon

Egg or oyster sauce can also be used for turbot or halibut, although the traditional sauce for them is a shrimp or lobster one.

Method
Put ingredients for court bouillon in a pan, salt lightly, cover and simmer for 8-10 minutes ; then leave to cool.

Tie fish in a piece of muslin, put in pan, cover and bring slowly to boil. Lower heat and barely simmer for 35-40 minutes. Take up and drain for 2-3 minutes before unwrapping muslin. Dish up on a hot dish and serve at once with your chosen sauce.

Egg sauce

This is a béchamel or white sauce, with the addition of chopped, hard-boiled egg. Put $\frac{3}{4}$ pint milk with 1 bayleaf, slice of onion, blade of mace and 6 peppercorns into a pan, infuse by covering and bringing slowly to scalding point. Pour off into a jug and cool slightly. Scrape out pan, melt 1 oz butter, gently stir in 1 rounded tablespoon plain flour off the heat, then strain on milk mixture about a third at a time. Season with salt and pepper. Blend well, then stir continually over heat until boiling. Boil for 1-2 minutes. Taste for seasoning then stir in 2 coarsely chopped hard-boiled eggs.

Oyster, shrimp or **lobster** sauce is made in the same way, but the fish is added in place of egg. A small tin of any of these shellfish is sufficient for the above amount of sauce.

Cod's roe pâté

12 oz smoked cod's roe (in the piece), or an 8 oz jar
1 teaspoon onion juice (from grated onion)
$\frac{1}{4}$ pint olive oil
1 cup fresh white breadcrumbs, or 3-4 slices of bread
1 packet Demi-Sel cheese
lemon, or tomato, juice (to taste)
pepper

To garnish
hot, dry toast
unsalted butter
black olives
lemon quarters

Method

Scarpe the roe from the skin and put it in a bowl with the onion juice. Pour the oil over the breadcrumbs and leave to soak for 5 minutes (if using slices of bread, remove the crust, put bread in a dish and sprinkle with the oil). Pound or beat the cod's roe with the Demi-Sel cheese until quite smooth, then work in the breadcrumbs and oil, a little at a time. Finish with lemon (or tomato) juice to taste and season with pepper. The mixture should be light and creamy.

Pile into a shallow dish and serve with hot dry toast (served between the folds of a napkin), unsalted butter, black olives and quarters of lemon in separate dishes.

1 *Scraping smoked cod's roe from the skin*
2 *Pounding the roe with Demi-Sel cheese*
3 *Dishing up the finished cod's roe pâté to serve as an hors d'œuvre*

28

Plaice

These flat sea-water fish are easily recognised because of their grey-brown skin and orange spots ; they weigh up to 5 lb. Eat when really fresh. Freshness is indicated by the brightness of the spots on the topside. Being rather tasteless, plaice need to be served with a well-flavoured sauce or savoury butter.

Fillets of plaice Sylvette

1 ½ -2 lb plaice (filleted and skinned)
salt
¼ pint water
squeeze of lemon juice
1 slice of onion
1 bayleaf
6 peppercorns

For vegetable mirepoix
4 oz carrots
2 oz onions
2 oz turnips
2 oz French beans, or brussels
   sprouts
1 stick of celery
2 tomatoes
salt and pepper
1 oz butter

For sauce
1 oz butter
1 rounded tablespoon plain flour
¼ pint creamy milk

Method

Set the oven at 350°F or Mark 4. To prepare vegetable mirepoix : dice all the vegetables finely, reserving the tomatoes. Melt 1 oz of the butter in a shallow pan and put in the diced vegetables, season and cover with a paper and lid. Cook gently for 3-4 minutes. Meanwhile scald and skin tomatoes, remove seeds and dice flesh ; add to the pan. Cover again and put the pan in the pre-set oven for about 20 minutes.

Wash the fish, lay it in a buttered ovenproof dish, sprinkle with salt and cover with the water and lemon juice. Add onion, bayleaf and peppercorns and poach in the coolest part of the oven for 15 minutes.

To make sauce ; melt the butter in a pan, blend in the flour away from the heat, strain on the liquor from the fish and blend. Stir over gentle heat until thick, add the creamy milk and simmer for 1-2 minutes.

Turn the vegetable mirepoix on to a serving dish, arrange the fillets on top and spoon over the sauce.

Haddock

This large, round sea-water fish, weighing from $1\frac{1}{2}$-6 lb, with firm white flakes, is in season all the year round. It is distinguishable by the dark line down each side and black 'finger' mark behind each gill, known as St. Peter's mark. Small fillets are sold as 'block' fillets and large ones are often smoked. The most sought after smaller haddock are split open and smoked ; these are known as Finnan haddock. Smaller whole fish, well smoked, are called Arbroath smokies.

Haddock au gratin

1-1$\frac{1}{2}$ lb fresh haddock fillet, or 4-5 $\frac{1}{2}$ block fillets according to size
salt and pepper
mushrooms (cooked and sliced)—
  optional

For sauce
1 oz butter
1 rounded tablespoon plain flour
$\frac{1}{2}$ pint milk
grated cheese
browned breadcrumbs

Method

Skin fillet and cut into portions ; lay flat in a buttered ovenproof dish. If using whole fillets, tuck each end under before laying in the dish. The side nearest the bone should be uppermost as this is always the whitest. Season lightly. Set oven at 350°F or Mark 4.

To prepare sauce : melt butter, stir in flour off the heat. Pour on milk, blend well, season and return to the heat. Stir continually until boiling. Taste for seasoning, then spoon sauce over the fish. Grate a little cheese over, scatter with browned crumbs, then bake in the pre-set oven for 20-25 minutes.

Cooked sliced mushrooms can be put over the fish before the sauce is spooned over, or they may be added to the sauce. **Watchpoint** The sauce for the fish cooked in this way should be thicker than an ordinary coating sauce to allow for dilution from the juices from the fish. The pieces of fish should be laid flat and completely cover the base of the dish, otherwise the liquid will not blend with the sauce and there will be a watery looking liquid round the edge of the dish.

Fish balls with tomato sauce

1½ lb fresh haddock fillet
8 oz fresh white breadcrumbs
salt and pepper
1 egg white
½ wineglass white wine
1 wineglass water
chopped parsley
½ - ¾ pint tomato sauce

Method

Skin and mince the fish, or work it in a blender and weigh ; there should be 1 lb. Set oven at 350°F or Mark 4.

Soak the breadcrumbs in cold water and squeeze dry in a piece of muslin, then work this panade into the fish with seasoning, adding the egg white gradually. When the mixture is really firm, shape it into pieces the size of marbles, and put these into a buttered ovenproof dish. Pour the white wine and water over the mixture, cover with foil and poach in pre-set oven for 15-20 minutes.

When cooked, remove foil and lift the fish balls carefully into hot serving dish ; add the chopped parsley to the tomato sauce and spoon it over the fish balls. These fish balls (known as 'boulettes') should be served hot.

Haddock with mushrooms

1-1½ lb fresh haddock fillet
5 tablespoons water
squeeze of lemon juice
salt

For sauce
2 oz mushrooms
1½ oz butter
1 dessertspoon paprika
black pepper (ground from mill)
1 rounded tablespoon plain flour
½ pint milk
1-2 caps pimiento (canned or fresh)
— cut into strips

Method

Set the oven at 350°F or Mark 4. Skin fillet and cut fish into 4-5 portions. Lay them in a buttered ovenproof dish, skinned side down, pour over the water and add the lemon juice. Salt lightly. Cover with buttered paper and poach for 15 minutes in the pre-set oven.

To prepare sauce : wash and slice mushrooms, cook for 2 minutes in half of the butter in a covered saucepan. Then draw pan aside, add paprika, pinch of salt, a dusting of black pepper and the rest of the butter.

Melt the butter, stir in the flour and blend in the milk off the heat. Stir until boiling, then draw pan aside.

Dish up the fish and strain the liquid into the sauce. Re-boil and reduce for 1-2 minutes. Then add pimiento and spoon sauce over the fish. Serve with noodles or pasta 'shells' tossed in a little melted butter.

Haddock Bercy

1-1½ lb fresh haddock fillets
salt
squeeze of lemon juice
¼ pint water
6 peppercorns
2 tomatoes
1 shallot (finely chopped)
1 wineglass dry white wine
kneaded butter (made with 1 oz
   butter and ½ oz plain flour)
1 dessertspoon chopped parsley
1 tablespoon double cream
bread for croûtes (optional)
garlic butter (optional)

Method

Set oven at 350°F or Mark 4.

Wash and dry fillets and place in a buttered ovenproof dish ; sprinkle with salt, add the lemon and water and put in the peppercorns. Cover with a buttered paper and poach in the pre-set oven for about 15 minutes or until tender.

Scald and skin the tomatoes, cut in four, remove the seeds and cut flesh into neat shreds ; keep on one side. Put the shallot in a pan with the wine, bring to the boil and reduce to half quantity. Strain on the liquid from the fish and thicken with the kneaded butter. Simmer for 2-3 minutes, adjust seasoning, add the parsley, cream and tomatoes and reheat gently.

Place the fish on a hot serving dish and spoon over the sauce. The dish may be garnished with crescent-shaped croûtes spread with garlic butter and toasted.

Shaped croûtes spread with garlic butter make an ideal garnish

Baked haddock with cream

1 lb fresh haddock (filleted) — or three block fillets
1 large onion (finely sliced)
1 oz butter
salt and pepper
1 small carton (2½ fl oz) double cream

For garnish (optional)
4 rashers streaky bacon (cut very thin)

Method

Set oven at 350°F or Mark 4. Wash and dry the fillets of fish and set on one side. Put the onion in a pan, cover with cold water, bring to the boil and then drain. Return onion to the saucepan with the butter, cover and cook very slowly until quite soft, yellow and buttery; do not let it brown. Place onion at the bottom of an ovenproof dish arrange the fish on the top, season lightly with salt and pepper and pour over the cream. Bake in the pre-set oven for about 10 minutes, until the cream has browned lightly on the top.

For a special occasion this dish can be garnished with very thin slices of fried streaky bacon.

Fillets of haddock florentine

1-1½ lb fresh haddock fillet (skinned)
salt
lemon juice
1 lb leaf spinach
½ oz butter

For mornay sauce
¾ oz butter
1 rounded tablespoon plain flour
½ pint milk
3 tablespoons grated cheese
salt and pepper
½ teaspoon made mustard (French, or English)

Method

Set oven at 350°F or Mark 4. Cut fillet into portions. Well butter an ovenproof dish, put in the fish and a little salt and sprinkle well with lemon juice. Cover with buttered paper and poach in the pre-set oven for 12 minutes.

Boil spinach, drain, press and return to pan with ½ oz butter. Toss over the heat for 1-2 minutes, then turn into an ovenproof serving dish. Arrange the fish on the top.

Prepare the mornay sauce (see method, page 138) reserving a little cheese. Pour sauce over fish to coat it, sprinkle with the reserved cheese and brown in oven at 425°F or Mark 7, or under grill.

Individual fish creams

¾ lb fresh haddock fillet
7½ fl oz thick béchamel sauce
1 egg
1 egg yolk
salt and pepper
2 oz shelled shrimps, or prawns
2 tablespoons cream
8-10 small mushrooms
squeeze of lemon juice
¼ oz butter

For white sauce
1 oz butter
1 oz plain flour
½ pint milk
salt and pepper

8-10 individual dariole moulds, or deep tartlet tins

Method
First prepare the béchamel sauce and turn on to a plate to cool.

Skin the fish, being careful to remove any bones, and pass the flesh twice through a mincer. Add the béchamel sauce gradually to fish and beat well. If preferred, this mixture can be put into a blender and worked for a few seconds only until it is thoroughly smooth. Then beat in the egg and extra yolk and season to taste. Add the shrimps or chopped prawns to this mixture with the cream.

Trim mushrooms and cook in 1 tablespoon of water and the lemon juice and butter.

Grease the moulds or tartlet tins. Place a mushroom in the bottom of each mould or tin and fill them to the brim with the cream. Cover each cream with a small piece of foil or buttered paper and steam or poach them au bain-marie for 10-15 minutes or until firm to the touch. Leave for 1-2 minutes before turning out creams. Have ready the white sauce and pour this around the fish creams.

Béchamel sauce is beaten into flaked haddock before the eggs, shrimps and cream are blended in

The moulds, with a mushroom at the bottom of each, are filled with fish mixture and poached au bain-marie

Mousseline
of fish

1½ lb fresh haddock fillet
3 egg whites (lightly broken)
½ pint double cream
salt and pepper
velouté, or suprême, sauce

Ring mould (1½ pints capacity)

This mousseline can also be
shaped into quenelles, or used
in quenelle moulds.

Method
Skin the fish, removing bones.
Mince the flesh twice and
weigh it ; there should be 1 lb.
Put minced mixture into a
bowl or blender ; work for 4-5
seconds, add the egg whites
gradually. Beat in the cream
by degrees, then add seasoning.
Watchpoint When making
this mousseline, be carefull not
to season until the egg whites
and cream have been worked in.
The consistency should be like
whipped cream ; but if it is at
all slack the addition of the salt
at this stage will stiffen it
immediately.

Turn mousseline into the
well-buttered mould and steam
or poach au bain-marie for
about 40-45 minutes or until
firm to the touch.

Leave mousseline for 3-4
minutes before turning out,
then pour over a velouté or
suprême sauce and serve hot.
Note : the sauce may be chosen
to taste ; eg. 2-3 oz chopped
prawns or shrimps can be added
to the velouté or suprême sauce.

Curried fish
croquettes

½ lb fresh haddock fillet
1 blade of mace
1 oz butter
1 shallot (finely chopped)
1 teaspoon curry powder
1 oz plain flour
4 fl oz milk
salt and pepper
½ egg (beaten)
deep fat (for frying)

For coating
1 egg (beaten)
dried white breadcrumbs

Method
Poach the haddock, with the
mace to flavour, in moderate
oven pre-set at 350°F or Mark
4, for 10-15 minutes or until
tender. Then drain, remove skin
and bones, and flake flesh. Melt
half the butter, add the shallot
and cook for 2-3 minutes. Add
the curry powder and cook for a
further minute. Blend in the
flour and milk, stir over heat
until boiling and allow to simmer for a minute or so. Put
flaked fish into the sauce a little
at a time. Season to taste and
add beaten egg. Turn mixture
on to a plate and allow it to get
quite cold. Divide it into dessert-
spoonfuls and roll into croquettes (cork shapes) on a
floured board. Coat with the
whole beaten egg and crumbs
and fry in deep fat until crisp
and golden-brown.

Omelet Arnold Bennett

4 eggs (separated)
4 tablespoons smoked haddock
(cooked and flaked)
2 oz butter
$\frac{1}{4}$ pint cream
salt and pepper
3 tablespoons grated Parmesan
cheese

This is an elegant dish which was created for the writer, Arnold Bennett, by the Savoy Grill in London. It is one of the best omelets.

Method

Toss the haddock with 1 oz butter and 2 tablespoons cream in a pan over a quick heat, for about 2-3 minutes, then leave it to cool.

Beat the egg yolks with 1 tablespoon cream and season. Whip the egg whites lightly, fold them into the yolks with the haddock and add half the cheese.

Melt the rest of the butter in the pan and cook omelet. Do not fold, but slide omelet on to a hot dish, sprinkle on rest of cheese and pour the cream over it. Brown quickly under a hot grill and serve at once.

To cook smoked haddock : cover the fish with water, and a dash of milk and bring slowly to the boil. Cover the pan, turn off the heat and leave for 10 minutes. Then drain the fish and remove the skin and any bones.

Far Eastern kedgeree

$\frac{1}{2}$ lb smoked haddock (cooked
and flaked)
2 hard-boiled eggs
4 oz long grain rice (boiled)
2 oz butter (melted)
black pepper
oil (for frying)
2 oz peanuts (weighed after
shelling and skinning)
$1\frac{1}{2}$ oz sultanas
chopped parsley

Method

Chop one hard-boiled egg. Fork the fish into the freshly boiled rice and add the melted butter and black pepper. Heat some oil and fry the peanuts to a pale gold, add the sultanas and continue frying for a few seconds to plump them. Add these to the fish and rice with the chopped egg. When ready to serve, pile on a dish, garnish with the sieved yolk of the second egg and then sprinkle on some chopped parsley.

Crêpes écossaises

For pancake batter
4 oz plain flour
pinch of salt
1 egg
1 egg yolk
$\frac{1}{2}$ pint milk
1 tablespoon melted butter

For filling
1 lb smoked haddock fillet
$\frac{1}{2}$ pint milk
2 eggs (hard-boiled)
$\frac{1}{2}$ small onion (sliced)
1 blade of mace
1$\frac{3}{4}$ oz butter
1$\frac{1}{2}$ oz plain flour
salt and pepper

To finish
1 oz butter (melted)
1 oz grated Parmesan cheese

Method

To make the batter : sift the flour with the salt into a bowl, make a well in the centre, add the egg and yolk and begin to add the milk slowly, stirring all the time. When half the milk has been added, stir in the melted butter and beat until smooth. Add remaining milk and leave batter to stand for 30 minutes.

Fry paper-thin pancakes, stacking one on top of the other. Wrap them in a clean dry teacloth until the filling is prepared.

Cover the smoked haddock with water, add 2 tablespoons of the milk, cover and bring slowly to the boil. Turn off the heat and leave for 10 minutes Then flake the fish, removing all the skin and any bones. Chop the hard-boiled eggs. Heat remaining milk with the onion and mace, tip into a jug, cover and leave to infuse. Rinse out the saucepan, melt the butter, blend in the flour, remove from the heat and strain on the milk. Return to the heat, stir until boiling and simmer for 3 minutes, draw pan aside, add the cooked fish and prepared eggs. Then adjust the seasoning.

Fill each pancake with a generous quantity of filling and place in a buttered gratin dish, or dishes. Brush well with melted butter and dust with the grated Parmesan cheese. Brown in the oven, pre-set at 375°F or Mark 5, for 7-10 minutes.
Note : the pancakes may be made in advance and kept in the refrigerator until required. In this case, do not brown them until just before serving.

Haddock with eggs

4 Finnan haddocks
4 eggs
½ pint milk
2 oz butter
1 large packet of frozen spinach
½ purée (thawed)
salt and pepper
squeeze of lemon juice

Method

Cut the fins and tails from the haddocks, wash fish and put into a pan. Pour over milk to cover and simmer for 7 minutes.

Meanwhile melt the butter in another pan, stir in the spinach purée, season and add a squeeze of lemon juice. Heat through gently and turn on to a warm serving dish, keep hot. Next poach the eggs, carefully keeping their shape. Drain the fish and set on top of the spinach purée, then place a poached egg on top of each fish. Serve very hot.

Poached eggs
(oeufs pochés)

New-laid eggs are best for poaching, otherwise the white will detach itself from the yolk. Poach eggs in a saucepan or deep frying pan filled with boiling water — add about 1 tablespoon vinegar to 1 quart of water. Do not add salt as this tends to toughen the white.

Keep heat low and water gently simmering then break eggs into pan and poach for about $3\frac{1}{2}$-$4\frac{1}{2}$ minutes until firm. Lift out with a draining spoon or fish slice and drain thoroughly before dishing up.

Haddock with eggs au gratin

4-5 eggs
1 lb finnan haddock
little milk
2 oz mushrooms
1 oz butter
salt and pepper
4-5 rounds of bread
oil (for frying croûtes)

For sauce
1 oz butter
1 rounded tablespoon plain flour
½ pint milk
2 tablespoons double cream
1 tablespoon grated Parmesan cheese
salt and pepper

Method

Poach eggs and keep them in a bowl of warm water while preparing other ingredients.

Trim the haddock, and cook (see page 36). Then flake with a fork ; set aside and keep warm.

Trim, wash and slice the mushrooms and put in a pan with the butter and seasoning ready for cooking. Fry the rounds of bread in hot oil until golden-brown ; drain them well.

To prepare the sauce : melt butter, stir in flour, blend in milk and bring to the boil. Simmer for 3 minutes, then beat in the cream and cheese. Taste sauce for seasoning.

Place the croûtes in a hot gratin dish, toss the prepared mushrooms over a quick heat for about 1 minute, mix in the haddock while the pan is still over the heat. Drain the eggs, arrange on the croûtes and scatter the haddock and mushroom mixture on top. Spoon over the sauce and glaze under the grill for 2-3 minutes.

Smoked haddock flan

For shortcrust pastry
6 oz plain flour
pinch of salt
1 oz shortening
3 oz butter
2 tablespoons cold water

For filling
1½ lb smoked haddock
(cooked and flaked — see page
36)
1½-2 lb potatoes (boiled and
creamed)
1 egg yolk
2 tablespoons grated cheese
1 small bunch of spring onions, or
green part of 1 leek (shredded,
well blanched)
2 hard-boiled eggs (quartered)

For béchamel sauce
½ pint milk (infused with slice of
onion, 6 peppercorns, 1 blade of
mace, 1 bayleaf)
¾ oz butter
1 rounded tablespoon plain flour
salt and pepper

8-inch diameter flan ring

Method

Make the shortcrust pastry and set aside to chill. When chilled, line pastry on to flan ring and bake blind for 20 minutes in the oven at 400°F or Mark 6.

Add the egg yolk to the creamed potato with 1 rounded tablespoon of grated cheese. Arrange flaked haddock on the pastry with onions on top and quartered hard-boiled eggs round the edge. Spoon the béchamel sauce over the top and decorate with creamed potato round the edge and across the centre (preferably using a forcing bag and an 8-cut rose pipe). Sprinkle with the rest of the grated cheese and brown in oven at 400-475°F or Mark 7 if filling is already hot. If filling is cold, heat flan for about 20-30 minutes at 350°F or Mark 4.

The flan is decorated with piped creamed potato which is then browned in the oven.

Smoked haddock quiche

For shortcrust pastry
8 oz plain flour
pinch of salt
4 oz shortening
2 oz butter
about 3-4 tablespoons water (to mix)

For filling
$\frac{1}{2}$ lb smoked haddock fillet
(cooked and flaked)
1 oz streaky bacon rashers
$\frac{1}{2}$ oz butter
1 egg
1 egg yolk
1 oz grated Cheddar cheese
$2\frac{1}{2}$ fl oz milk
$2\frac{1}{2}$ fl oz single cream
pepper (ground from mill)
salt (optional)

8-inch diameter flan ring

Method

First make the pastry and chill for about 15 minutes. Then roll out and line flan ring. Set oven at 375°F of Mark 5.

Remove the rind from the bacon and cut into thin strips. Cook in a pan with the butter until frizzled. Beat the whole egg and yolk with the cheese and milk in a bowl; pour this over the cooked flaked haddock and add the bacon and cream. Season with a little pepper, but taste the mixture before adding any salt as it is quite possible that the haddock, cheese and bacon will make the filling salty enough.

Put mixture in the pastry-lined flan ring and bake in pre-set oven until the filling is set and the top is golden-brown (about 25 minutes).

Watchpoint As this filling is made with egg it is important that the oven is not too hot. To make sure that the pastry is well baked on the underside, place a baking sheet in the oven while pre-heating and then place the flan on top for baking; this will give extra bottom heat.

Pike

A fresh-water fish with white, friable flesh, a long head, scaly body and fins placed towards its tail end, this fish can grow up to 30 lb, but those normally eaten weigh about 5 lb. They may be grilled or fried, but are best baked with a well-flavoured stuffing, as in the recipe below.

Roast pike

1 medium-size pike (2½-3 lb)
3-4 oz butter
¼ pint brown ale
scant ¼ pint water

For stuffing
2 onions (finely chopped)
2 oz butter
4 oz fresh white breadcrumbs
3 rounded tablespoons chopped parsley
1 rounded tablespoon chopped mixed herbs
grated rind and juice of 1 lemon
6 anchovy fillets (pounded), or
   1 tablespoon anchovy essence
1-2 eggs (beaten)
salt and pepper

This particular recipe is a Cumberland one, made with locally caught pike. Fresh haddock can be used instead of pike. If preferred, red or white wine can be used in place of ale.

Method

Well wash and scale the pike after gutting. Brush the stomach cavity to make sure it is thoroughly clean and remove the head. Set oven at 350°F or Mark 4.

Soften the onion in the butter, then turn it into a bowl. Add breadcrumbs, herbs, lemon rind and juice and pounded anchovy (or anchovy essence). Bind with enough egg to make a moist but not too wet stuffing. Season well with pepper, and a little salt if necessary. Stuff the pike with the mixture and sew up, or fasten with small skewers and lace with string. Spread a doubled sheet of greaseproof paper thickly with about half the butter. Curl the pike round in a roasting tin, tuck the buttered paper over and round it. Put the rest of the butter in the tin with the ale and water.

Cook in the pre-set oven for 30-35 minutes. Then remove paper, increase the heat to 375°F or Mark 5 and continue to cook, basting frequently, for another 20-25 minutes. The skin should be nicely crisp and brown. As pike is a dry fish it is important to keep it well basted during cooking. Serve with a sauce or savoury butter, eg. anchovy or tomato. The juices from the pan are poured over the fish before serving.

Skate

This flat sea-water fish has become much more popular in recent years and therefore more expensive. At one time it was seldom seen outside fried fish shop ; now it is in most fishmongers. The flesh is creamy white, very digestible and excellent in flavour. Skate is at its best from August to April. As a whole fish it is extremely ugly and the only parts that are sold are the side pieces or 'wings'. Each wing weighs $1\frac{1}{2}$-$2\frac{1}{2}$ lb ; the underside is white, the upper side mottled brown and black. Do not eat when very fresh as flesh is too tough.

After cooking, both skins are removed. At first sight the wing may seem full of bones but these are really a gelatinous gristle and are easily removed on the plate. The best methods of cooking are deep fat frying or poaching in a court bouillon.

Skate au gratin

2 lb wing of skate
court bouillon (see page 20), or
    water plus 1-2 tablespoons
    vinegar
about 16 button onions
$\frac{1}{2}$ oz butter
1 teaspoon granulated sugar
triangular pieces of bread
    (for croûtes)
oil (for frying)

For sauce
$\frac{3}{4}$ pint milk (infused with 1 slice of
    onion, 1 blade of mace, 4-5
    peppercorns, few parsley stalks)
1 oz butter
1 rounded tablespoon plain flour
salt and pepper
2 oz cheese (grated)

Method
First make court bouillon, then set aside. Cut skate into fingers, put in a shallow pan and cover with court bouillon, or water and vinegar. Simmer for 20 minutes. Draw pan aside.

To prepare sauce : heat and infuse milk and then pour into a jug. Melt butter in the pan used for flavouring milk, stir in flour off the heat and cook to a pale straw colour. Strain on the milk, blend and stir until boiling. Draw pan aside, adding seasoning and three-quarters of the cheese, a little at a time. Set sauce aside.

Blanch onions, drain and return to the pan with $\frac{1}{2}$ oz butter and 1 teaspoon sugar. Cover and cook for 5-7 minutes until golden-brown and tender. Shake pan occasionally. Fry bread in oil until brown.

Drain pieces of skate, remove skin and arrange in an oven-proof dish, spoon over the sauce, sprinkle on the remaining cheese and brown in the oven at 425°F or Mark 7 for 7-10 minutes. Serve garnished with the glazed onions and croûtes.

Skate in black butter

1-2 wings of skate (weighing about 2 lb in all)
court bouillon (as recipe on page 20 but with double the amount of vinegar)

For black butter
2-3 oz butter
1 tablespoon capers
1 dessertspoon chopped parsley
5 tablespoons wine vinegar
salt and pepper

Method

Have ready the court bouillon. Strain into a comparatively shallow pan such as a deep frying pan with a lid. Well wash the skate and cut into wedges ; the bone looks tough but is quite easy to cut through. Put fish into warm stock, cover, bring slowly to boil and simmer gently for 15-20 minutes. Lift out fish, drain on muslin, or absorbent paper, and gently scrape away any skin. Place on a hot dish, slide into oven to keep hot.

To make black butter : pour off the stock, reheat the pan, drop in the butter and cook to a rich brown (not black) colour. Spoon quickly over the fish, season, if necessary, then scatter over the capers and parsley. Add vinegar to the pan and reduce quickly by half. Pour over the dish and serve very hot with plain, boiled potatoes.

Poached wings of skate in black butter with a garnish of capers

Sole

Considered the best of white fish, there are two main varieties, Dover (or black) sole, which is the most prized and most expensive, and the lemon sole. Both are flat sea-water fish, the Dover sole with a brownish-black skin and rather narrow shape and the lemon a paler, more sandy brown and a larger oval in shape.

Lemon soles weigh from 1-2 lb and, after skinning on both sides, may be grilled whole, or filleted and served fried meunière (in foaming butter with beurre noisette poured over), or poached and coated with various sauces.

Small Dover or black soles, weighing 8-12 oz, are known as 'slip' soles. Skinned on both sides, they may be grilled, fried, or boned and stuffed. Soles are available all year round but at their best from April to January.

Preparation of fillets

Batting out

First skin and trim the fillet. Place it between two pieces of waxed, or dampened grease-proof paper, the side nearest the bone uppermost. Take a small, heavy frying pan or saucepan and, holding it in both hands, bring it down smartly on to the length of the fillet until it has spread out by about $\frac{1}{4}$ inch.

This batting breaks the fibres and prevents the fish from shrinking too much during cooking. Care must be taken to do this batting out evenly and not to overdo it. The pan is a substitute for a cutlet bat, which is the most suitable instrument to use but rare to find in most kitchens as it is a specialist's tool.

Next fold fillet over, skinned side underneath, before poaching, or, if it is to be stuffed, spread the stuffing on the skinned side and then carefully reshape fillet.

Folding

This process is especially important when cooking any advanced recipe using filleted fish. Careful and neat folding makes a vast difference to the appearance of the finished dish.

Fold the fillets once over, skinned side underneath ; keep the tail half on the top and tuck the tip under, making sure that all the fillets are the same length. This may mean less of the top part of two fillets being tucked underneath in order to even them out.

Sole Caprice

Where fish is served as a main course, a double fillet may be either folded in two as below, or folded over lengthways.

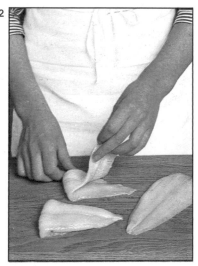

2 **Dover soles (1¼ lb each) — filleted**
4-6 **oz butter (melted)**
2 **cups fresh white breadcrumbs**
2 **bananas**
lemon juice
½ **pint tomato sauce (well seasoned)**

Method
Have the fillets ready skinned, washed and dried. Draw them through the melted butter, then through the crumbs, which should be on a sheet of paper, pressing them well on to the fillets with a palette knife. Set fillets on grid of grill pan, baste well with melted butter and grill them gently for 10-12 minutes. Keep hot.

Peel the bananas, then slice them diagonally into four ; sauté them quickly in the remaining butter with a little lemon juice until golden-brown.

Arrange a slice of banana on each fillet, dish up and serve very hot, with the tomato sauce separately.

Watchpoint The tomato sauce should be made with the minimum of flour so that it is clear, red and not too thick.

1 *To fold a fillet in three, tuck under tail and head end*
2 *To fold fillet in two, bring the head end to meet the tail*

Sole andalouse

4 **double fillets of sole, or plaice**
¼ **pint water**
squeeze of lemon juice
4 **large tomatoes**
2-3 **tablespoons olive oil**

For dressing
5-6 **tablespoons olive oil**
2 **tablespoons wine vinegar**
¼ **pint fresh tomato sauce**
  (made from ¾ lb tomatoes,
  1-2 teaspoons tomato purée,
  1 clove of garlic, pared rind
  and juice of ½ lemon, salt and
  pepper, sugar to taste)
1 **tablespoon mixed chopped**
  herbs (parsley, chives, thyme)

For decoration
anchovy fillets
watercress (optional)

Method

Set oven at 350°F or Mark 4. Skin the double fillets, fold them in half and poach in the water with the lemon juice in pre-set oven for about 15 minutes. Cool them in the liquid, then drain well.

Meanwhile scald and skin tomatoes, cut in half and flick out the seeds. Heat 2-3 tablespoons of oil in a frying pan, fry the tomatoes very quickly for 1 minute only, then drain. Arrange on the serving dish and place each fillet across two halves.

To prepare the dressing: combine oil, vinegar and tomato sauce and adjust the seasoning. Add the herbs, spoon dressing over the fillets and decorate each one with anchovy fillets. Garnish with watercress if liked. Serve cold as a first course.

1

2

1 *Oil, vinegar and tomato sauce are whisked together, and fresh herbs are added, to make the dressing*
2 *The sole fillets, arranged on tomato halves, are decorated with anchovy fillets after the tomato dressing has been spooned over*

Fillets of sole (or plaice) andalouse make a good first course for a dinner party particularly in warm weather. Garnish with sprigs of crisp watercress

Sole à la Jouy

2 soles (1 lb each) — filleted

For court bouillon
2 wineglasses white wine
$\frac{1}{4}$ pint water
bones and trimmings from soles
1 blade of mace
2 allspice berries
bouquet garni
salt and pepper

For sauce
$1\frac{1}{2}$ oz butter
$1\frac{1}{4}$ oz plain flour
$\frac{1}{2}$ pint court bouillon
2 egg yolks
2 good tablespoons double cream
$2\frac{1}{2}$ fl oz fresh tomato pulp (see
  method, page 50), or sauce, or $\frac{1}{2}$
  teaspoon tomato purée
$\frac{1}{4}$ lb button mushrooms (sliced
  and sautéd in $\frac{1}{2}$ oz butter)

Method
Place the bones and fish trimmings in a pan with all the ingredients for court bouillon ; simmer gently for 20-30 minutes, then strain and reserve liquid. Set oven at 350°F or Mark 4. Wash and dry fillets, place in a buttered ovenproof dish, cover with a little of the court bouillon and poach in pre-set oven for about 8-10 minutes.

To prepare sauce : melt the butter, add flour and cook gently until it is a pale straw colour ; blend in $\frac{1}{2}$ pint of court bouillon and stir until boiling. Mix the egg yolks and cream, then add to the sauce off the heat. Add the tomato pulp (or sauce or purée) and cooked mushrooms.

Dish up the fillets on a hot serving dish, spoon over the sauce and serve.

Sole Maintenon

2 soles ($1\frac{1}{4}$ lb each) — filleted
  and skinned
12 oz mushrooms (cup, or
  button)
2 shallots
$\frac{1}{2}$ oz butter
2 wineglasses white wine
salt and pepper
$\frac{1}{2}$ wineglass water
approximately $2\frac{1}{2}$ fl oz double cream
kneaded butter
1 tablespoon grated Parmesan
  cheese

Method
Set oven at 350°F or Mark 4.

Wash the mushrooms, chop them finely ; chop the shallots and cook them in butter for 3-5 minutes. Add mushrooms and, after 1-2 minutes, half the wine. Season and cook briskly for 5 minutes, uncovered.

Turn this mixture into an ovenproof gratin dish, arrange fillets on top, pour over the remaining wine and water. Poach fish in pre-set oven for 10-15 minutes.

When fish is cooked, carefully strain off the liquor and reduce it by one-third. Keep fish warm.

Measure liquor and take half its amount in cream.

Watchpoint When the liquor from the fish is reduced, there should be just over $\frac{1}{4}$ pint, so approximately $2\frac{1}{2}$ fl oz cream are needed.

Mix both together, bring to the boil, draw pan aside and add enough kneaded butter to thicken sauce. Reboil it and simmer for 3-5 minutes, then season. Spoon this sauce over the poached fish, sprinkle with grated Parmesan cheese and brown under grill. Serve at once.

Fillets of sole meunière

2 Dover soles (each weighing
   1½ lb) — filleted
2 tablespoons seasoned flour
4 rashers of short back, or
   streaky, bacon
3 oz butter
juice of ½ small lemon
salt and pepper
1 dessertspoon chopped mixed
   herbs

Method
Skin the fillets if this has not
been done by your fishmonger,
then wash and dry them thoroughly. Just before you are
ready to start cooking, roll the
fillets in seasoned flour.

Meanwhile grill or fry the
bacon until crisp and golden;
lift it on to absorbent paper
and keep it warm.

Watchpoint Have your serving
dish hot and ready before you
start cooking, as fish à la
meunière is never drained but
always put straight on to the
serving dish.

Heat the frying pan, drop in
about one-third of the butter and
as it foams put in the fish, skin
side uppermost; fry on both
sides until golden-brown. Arrange fish on the serving dish
with a rasher of bacon between
every two fillets.

Wipe out the pan, drop in the
remaining butter and cook it
gently until nut-brown, then add
the lemon juice, with the
seasoning and the herbs. Rotate
the pan quickly to blend the
butter and juice; when this is
foaming pour it over the fish.
Serve at once.

Fillets of sole Dorothea

2 soles (1¼-1½ lb each) — filleted
squeeze of lemon juice
salt

For sauce
1 oz butter
1 oz plain flour
7½ fl oz milk (flavoured as for
   béchamel)
1 small carton (about 2½ fl oz)
   double cream
1 rounded teaspoon chopped truffle
   (optional)

For rice
5-6 oz long grain rice
1 small onion (finely chopped)
1 oz butter
good pinch of saffron (infused in 2
   tablespoons hot water)
½ pint fresh tomato pulp (well
   seasoned and flavoured)
about ¾-1 pint of good chicken,
   or veal, stock

Savarin, or ring, mould (2 pints
capacity)

Method

Set oven at 350°F or Mark 4.
Butter the mould well, then prepare the rice. Soften the onion in the butter in a flame-proof casserole, stir in the rice and cook gently for a few minutes. Then add the saffron, half the tomato pulp and three-quarters of the stock. Season, bring to the boil, cover and put in pre-set oven.

After 10 minutes, look at the rice and add a little more of the stock if necessary. Return the casserole to the oven for a further 5 minutes, when the rice should be dry and flaky.

Fill the prepared mould with the rice, press down lightly and keep warm.

Meanwhile skin the fillets, fold in two and lay them in a buttered ovenproof dish. Pour over enough water to cover them, add a squeeze of lemon and a little salt, cover and poach in the oven for about 10-15 minutes.

While the fish is cooking prepare the sauce. Make a béchamel sauce with the butter, flour and milk in the usual way, and finish with the cream. Stir in enough of the remaining tomato pulp to give it a delicate tomato flavour and add the truffle.

Turn out the rice in the centre of a round silver or steel dish, surround with the fillets of sole slightly overlapping and coat with the sauce. Serve at once.

To make tomato pulp In season use rather ripe tomatoes. At other times of the year it is better to use canned Italian tomatoes. To make ½ pint take ¾ lb ripe tomatoes (seeds removed) or a 14 oz can of tomatoes. Put into a pan with a clove of lightly bruised garlic, a bayleaf, salt, and pepper from the mill and a slice of onion. Add a nut of butter, cover and cook slowly to a thick pulp, about 10-15 minutes. When really thick, pass through a strainer. Adjust the seasoning ; add a little sugar if necessary. The pulp should not be sharp.

Sole with cider

1¼-1½ lb sole (filleted)
1½ wineglasses dry cider
½ wineglass water
1 oz butter
1 rounded dessertspoon plain
flour
squeeze of lemon juice
1 dessertspoon chopped parsley
1-2 tablespoons single cream

This sauce is especially good
with sole but also goes well
with brill.

Method
Fold the fillets, skinned side
under, and lay on an ovenproof
dish rubbed with a little of the
butter. Pour over the cider and
water, cover with buttered paper
and poach in the oven, pre-set
at 350°F or Mark 4, for 12-15
minutes.
  Melt the rest of the butter in
a saucepan. Stir in the flour off
the heat. Strain on the liquor
from the sole, blend, return pan
to heat and bring to the boil.
Simmer for 3-4 minutes. Add
lemon juice, parsley and cream.
Put fish in clean serving dish,
coat with the sauce and serve
at once.

Sole janvier

2 soles (each weighing 1¼ lb
filleted)
6 oz white mushrooms
½ lb ripe tomatoes (skinned,
seeds removed, and sliced)
salt and pepper
1 wineglass white wine

For sauce
1 oz butter
½ oz plain flour
¼ pint double cream

Method
Set oven at 350°F or Mark 4.
  Skin, wash and dry the fillets.
Wash and trim the mushrooms
and slice them thinly. Lay the
mushrooms and tomatoes in a
well-buttered ovenproof dish,
season, and arrange the fillets
on top. Pour over the wine and
cover with a thickly buttered
paper. Poach in pre-set moderate oven for about 15 minutes.
  Lift the fillets into a hot
serving dish and keep warm.
Tip the tomatoes, mushrooms
and liquor from the cooking
dish into a pan ; work half the
butter with the flour and add
it to the pan in small pieces.
Reboil, stirring well, and reduce
a little. Add the cream and boil
up well. Draw pan aside and
stir in the remaining butter.
Spoon sauce over the fish and
brown under a hot grill.

Fillets of sole Dugléré

1½ lb sole (filleted, with bone)
½ pint fish stock (made with 1 shallot,
   6 peppercorns, 1 bayleaf, salt)

For sauce
2 tomatoes (ripe and firm)
1 oz butter
1 rounded tablespoon plain flour
stock from fish
4-5 tablespoons single cream, or
   top of milk
salt and pepper
1 dessertspoon chopped parsley

This dish is a classic and best made with Dover or lemon sole. For a main course, allow 2 fillets per person.

> **Fillet of sole Dugléré** was named after the French chef Dugléré who used to work at the famous Café Anglais in Paris (no longer in existence).

Method

First make stock. Break fish bone into 2-3 pieces, put into a pan with shallot, peppercorns and bayleaf. Pour on ½ pint water, add a little salt then simmer, covered, for 20 minutes. Strain and cool. Set oven at 350°F or Mark 4.

Skin fillets, if not already done by the fishmonger, then wash and dry. Fold them over, skinned side under and the tail end on top to make the fillet slightly pointed. Lay in a buttered ovenproof dish and pour over stock. Cover with buttered paper or foil, poach in pre-set oven for 10-12 minutes.

Scald, skin and quarter tomatoes. Cut away stalk from each quarter, flick out seeds. Cut lengthways into three strips. Then melt the butter, blend in the flour and cook for 2-3 seconds to make a roux, then draw aside. Take up the fish, dish up and keep warm. Strain the stock on to the roux, blend, return to the heat and stir until thickening. Then add cream or milk, season and bring to the boil. Simmer 1-2 minutes, then add tomatoes and parsley. Spoon the sauce over the fillets at once.

This sauce is a velouté and is made with a lightly cooked roux. The liquid should always be stock with cream or creamy milk added at end; if fish has been poached in fish stock, this makes for a better sauce, but you can use plain water with sliced shallot and backbone laid on top.

Whiting

These round, sea-water fish are light and silvery in colour, weighing from $\frac{1}{2}$-1 lb. The delicate flesh is apt to crumble and is easy to digest.

Whiting alsacienne

4 large whiting fillets (1$\frac{1}{2}$ lb)
1 small firm cabbage
2 oz butter
1 onion (finely sliced)
salt and pepper
1 bayleaf
2$\frac{1}{2}$ fl oz water
1 rounded tablespoon plain flour
7$\frac{1}{2}$ fl oz milk
1 oz dry Cheddar cheese (grated)
1 tablespoon grated Parmesan cheese — to finish

Method
Cut the cabbage into quarters, removing hard stalk, and shred finely. Melt half the butter in a wide-based flameproof casserole, put in sliced onion ; cover, cook for 2-3 minutes, then add the cabbage. Season, cover and cook slowly until soft (15-20 minutes for green cabbage, up to 50 minutes for white). Set oven at 350°F or Mark 4.

Fold the fillets, lay in a buttered ovenproof dish, add the bayleaf, seasoning and water. Poach in the pre-set oven for about 15 minutes.

Make a cheese sauce (using remaining butter), adding liquor from fish before the milk.

Lay the cabbage in a clean ovenproof dish, arrange the fish on the top and spoon over the sauce. Sprinkle with the Parmesan cheese and brown slowly under the grill.

Whitings Orly

3-4 whitings (about 12 oz filleted)
squeeze of lemon juice
seasoned flour
$\frac{1}{2}$-$\frac{3}{4}$ pint fritter batter
deep fat (for frying)

The name Orly denotes food, usually slices of fish or meat, coated with rich batter and fried in deep fat.

Method
Skin the fillets, lay them on a plate and sprinkle lightly with a little lemon juice. Leave in the refrigerator for about 1 hour. Then dab the fillets with absorbent paper to dry and cut each one into diagonal strips about 1 inch or more in width.

To fry the whiting, first roll them in seasoned flour. Have the batter ready. Heat the fat bath until at frying temperature. To test heat if you have no thermometer, drop in 1-inch cube of bread ; it should turn golden-brown in 20 seconds in oil, and 40 seconds in solid fats. Put a few pieces of the fish into the batter. Turn round lightly with a flat whisk or fork, lift out and drop carefully into the fat. Fry about 6-8 pieces at a time ; when golden-brown, lift out and drain on absorbent paper or a cooling rack set over a baking sheet, then set aside. Continue until all the pieces of fish are fried, dish up and serve either a sweet pimiento sauce, or a tartare sauce, separately. Serve as a first course.

Sweet pimiento sauce

2 egg yolks
1 hard-boiled egg yolk (sieved)
½ teaspoon paprika pepper
salt and pepper
dash of Tabasco sauce
grated rind of ½ orange
7½ fl oz olive, or salad, oil
about 1 dessertspoon vinegar
    (to taste)
2 small caps of canned pimiento
    (or 1 large one) — finely chopped,
    or rubbed through a sieve
1 tablespoon juice from
    pimiento can
1 tablespoon double cream
    (optional)

Method

Put the egg yolks, both raw and hard-boiled, into a bowl. Work with the seasonings and orange rind, then gradually add the oil as if making mayonnaise. When it begins to get too thick, add the vinegar. When all the oil is mixed in, add the chopped strained pimientos. Finish with the juice and the cream, if used, and adjust seasoning.

Whitings Orly may be served with pimiento sauce or tartare sauce

Bass

These are beautiful, round, silvery fish not often seen on the fishmonger's slab but well worth asking for.

In season from May to July, they weigh from 2-6 lb. Like salmon, bass are 'fighting' fish and so have crisp firm flesh. They may be both fresh- and sea-water fish and are more likely to be found in the south and west parts of the country, the estuaries of south Devon and Cornwall being among the major fishing grounds.

Small bass may be grilled or fried but the larger fish or steaks cut from them are best poached (see method for poaching brill with mushrooms and prawns) and served with a hollandaise sauce or cooked as for salmon.

Brill

Medium to large flat sea-water fish having a pale brown skin with flesh of a creamy colour, firm and of good flavour. Brill weigh 2-6 lb and they are at their best and most easily obtainable from September to May. Cook filleted or whole and serve with a good sauce and garnishes, and with cucumber.

Brill with onions

1½-2 lb brill (filleted)
½-¾ cup of water
squeeze of lemon juice
salt and pepper
½ lb onions
1 oz butter

For sauce
¾ oz butter
1 rounded tablespoon plain flour
¼ pint creamy milk
salt and pepper
1 teaspoon French mustard
1-2 tablespoon grated Cheddar
  cheese

Method
Set the oven at 350°F or Mark 4. Skin fillets and cut in half diagonally. Put on a buttered ovenproof dish, pour over the water and add a good squeeze of lemon juice. Season, cover with buttered paper or foil and poach fish in pre-set oven for 10-12 minutes.

Slice onions very thinly and push out into rings. Melt butter in a shallow saucepan, add onions, press a piece of buttered paper or foil on top and cover tightly with a lid. Cook slowly until soft, about 10-12 minutes. Turn onions on to a serving dish and keep warm.

To prepare sauce : melt butter in a pan, stir in the flour off the heat, then pour in the liquid from the fish. Blend and thicken slightly over gentle heat. Then pour in the milk, stir sauce until boiling. Season to taste and cook for 1-2 minutes. Draw aside. Arrange fish on top of the onions. Stir the mustard and half the cheese into the sauce ; pour this over dish. Sprinkle the rest of the cheese on top and brown under the grill. Serve very hot.

Brill with mushrooms and prawns

1½-2 lb brill (filleted)
4 oz button mushrooms (sliced)
1½ wineglasses of white wine, or fish
   stock made from the bones
salt and pepper
4-5 tomatoes (skinned and
   thinly sliced)
½ oz butter
parsley (chopped)

For sauce
1 shallot (finely chopped)
1 oz butter
1 rounded tablespoon plain flour
½ pint milk
2 tablespoons double cream
3-4 oz shelled prawns (coarsely
   chopped)

Method

Set the oven at 325-350°F or Mark 3-4. Well butter an ovenproof dish. Skin the fillets and cut in half diagonally. Arrange them in the dish with the mushroom slices scattered on top. Pour over the wine or stock, season and cover with thickly buttered paper. Poach in the pre-set oven for 15 minutes.

Meanwhile, place the tomato slices down the centre of another ovenproof dish (in which the fish will finally be served), dot with butter and cover with buttered paper. Put into the oven with the fish for 5-7 minutes.

Take up fish, arrange fillets on tomatoes and keep warm.

Make sauce : pour fish liquor into a pan, add chopped shallot and boil hard to reduce to 2-3 tablespoons. Pour off and set aside. Then, in the same pan, melt butter, stir in flour and pour on the milk. Return pan to heat and stir until boiling, making sure there are no lumps ; season, and boil hard to reduce a little. Add fish liquor and shallot mixture, bring to boil and simmer for a few seconds. Add the chopped prawns and cream ; season, if necessary. Then spoon the sauce over the fish and sprinkle with chopped parsley.

Brill with cucumber

4-6 fillets of brill (1½-2 lb)
rind and juice of ½ lemon
¼ pint water
salt
peppercorns
1 large cucumber (peeled and
    cut in chunks)
½ oz butter
dill, or mint, or parsley (chopped)
1 dessertspoon grated cheese

For sauce
1 oz butter
1 rounded tablespoon plain flour
¼ pint milk
salt and pepper

Method

Set oven at 325°F or Mark 3. Wash, skin and dry fillets. Fold the ends of the fillets under, put in a buttered flameproof dish, pour on the lemon juice and water and grate over a little lemon rind. Season with salt and a few peppercorns, cover with buttered greaseproof paper and poach in pre-set oven for 15-20 minutes, or until tender. Strain the fish and reserve the liquor.

Peel cucumber, cut into chunks and drop into boiling salted water for 1 minute, then drain. Melt a good ½ oz butter, add the cucumber and season to taste. Cover and simmer until almost tender (about 5 minutes). Add the dill, mint or parsley.

To make sauce : melt the butter in another pan, remove pan from heat and blend in the flour and the strained liquor from the fish. Stir the sauce over gentle heat until thickening, then add milk. Bring to the boil and reduce rapidly to the consistency of cream. Taste for seasoning.

Dish up the fish, pour over the sauce, sprinkle with the cheese and brown lightly under the grill. Garnish with the cucumber. Serve as a first course.

Brill makes a good first course when served with white sauce and cucumber

Red mullet

These much esteemed round sea-water fish have delicate white flesh with a bright pink, fairly thick skin. They average between 6-12 oz in weight and are in season from May to September. The fishmonger, if asked, will clean them through the gills and leave in the liver, which is considered a delicacy to be cooked in the fish. For this reason red mullet is called the 'woodcock of the sea' (this prized game bird being dressed without being drawn or cleaned). Red mullet can also be cleaned as for other fish, if preferred.

A famous method of cooking them is 'en papillote', that is wrapped in an envelope of well-buttered greaseproof paper. In this way all the flavour of the fish is preserved. Red mullet can also be fried or grilled and served with a maître d'hôtel butter.

Grey mullet

In appearance these round sea-water fish bear no relationship to red mullet. The fish are large, weighing from 2-3 lb upwards and are caught off the Cornish coast from spring to late summer. The flesh is beautifully white and firm, the skin silvery-grey. Cook as for salmon, sliced and grilled, or poached and served with a sauce such as hollandaise, or one made from the poaching liquid, eg. Dugléré.

Red mullet duxelles

4 red mullet (cleaned)
2 wineglasses red wine, or fish stock and squeeze of lemon juice
quarters of lemon (to garnish)

For duxelles
6 oz mushrooms, or mushroom stalks
1 oz butter
1 tablespoon finely chopped shallots, or onion
2 tablespoons chopped parsley

Method
Set oven at 350°F or Mark 4.

To make duxelles : wash mushrooms and chop finely. Cook with shallots and parsley in melted butter for 3-5 minutes, until most of the moisture has evaporated. Turn into a buttered ovenproof dish, spreading the mixture evenly. Lay mullet on top and pour over wine or stock (if no wine, add a squeeze of lemon juice). Cook in the pre-set oven for 15-20 minutes, basting occasionally. When ready the liquid should be well reduced.

Garnish with quarters of lemon and serve with boiled potatoes.

Duxelles denotes a mixture of mushrooms, shallots and herbs. The term may have originated in the kitchens of the 17th-century Marquis d'Uxelles, a gastronome renowned for his book on French cookery.

Red mullet 'en papillote'

4 red mullet (cleaned)
2½ oz butter
salt
black pepper (ground from mill)
lemon juice
extra butter (for melting) —
   optional

Method
Set oven at 350°F or Mark 4.

Cut an oval of greaseproof paper for each fish (large enough to enclose it), spread the centre well with butter, place a fish on each and season well, adding a good squeeze of lemon juice. Wrap up the fish, crimping the edges of the paper together by making small 'pleats' in it (see photographs).

Slide on to a baking sheet and cook in the pre-set oven for 15-18 minutes.

To serve, unwrap the papers carefully and slide fish on to a hot dish or individual plates. Serve a little melted butter separately, if wanted.

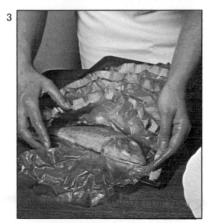

1 *Red mullet 'en papillote' : fish is placed on greased paper and lemon juice is added*
2 *Crimping edges of the paper 'envelope' to seal it so that juices do not escape*
3 *Unwrapping the cooked red mullet 'en papillote' ; serve with melted butter*

Red mullet niçoise

4 red mullet
2 tablespoons olive oil
1 clove of garlic (finely chopped)
1 teaspoon paprika pepper
1 teaspoon tomato purée
1 wineglass white wine
a sprig of thyme
salt
pepper (ground from mill)
4 oz black olives (stoned)
quarters of lemon

Method
Heat the olive oil in a small pan, add the garlic and the paprika pepper and cook slowly until soft. Remove from heat, add the tomato purée and moisten with the wine. Set oven at 350°F or Mark 4.

Wash the fish and remove the gills, dry and place in a large ovenproof dish with a sprig of thyme, then season. Spoon over the sauce and cook in the pre-set oven for 15-20 minutes, basting well.

Add the stoned black olives to the mullet when cooked and replace in the oven to heat through. Serve with quarters of lemon. This dish is also good cold.

Turbot

This is one of the finest white fish, with firm white flesh and a gelatinous skin. Turbot can grow to an enormous size, but small fish, known as chicken turbot, weighing about 6 lb, can be bought whole or filleted.

Turbot steaks with shrimp sauce

2 turbot steaks (4-6 oz each)
squeeze of lemon juice
salt
4 tablespoons water

For shrimp sauce
$\frac{1}{2}$ oz butter
$\frac{1}{2}$ oz plain flour
1 small carton of potted shrimps
salt and pepper
$7\frac{1}{2}$ fl oz flavoured milk
1 tablespoon cream (optional)

Method
Set oven at 350°F or Mark 4. Wash fish and dry in absorbent paper. Sprinkle lightly with lemon juice and salt and lift into a buttered ovenproof dish; add water and poach for 10-15 minutes in the pre-set oven.

To make the shrimp sauce: melt the butter, add the flour off the heat and pour on the flavoured milk; blend and stir until boiling. Cook for 2-3 minutes then remove from heat.

Remove a little of the surplus butter from the top of the shrimps and discard, then add the remainder of the butter and the shrimps to sauce. Adjust the seasoning and reheat gently, but do not boil. If wished the sauce can be finished with cream; serve sauce separately.

Halibut

A flat, North Atlantic fish, this can weigh anything from 2 lb — 400 lb and grow to 10 feet long.

'Chicken' halibut (2-5 lb), in season from March to October, have the best flavour. Larger ones, sold in steaks or pieces, are best from August to April. They can replace cod or turbot in many dishes, such as the one below.

Chiorro

1½ lb halibut (divided into cutlets)
3 tablespoons butter, or oil
4 large onions (thinly sliced)
12 cloves of garlic (very finely chopped)
1 rounded teaspoon tomato purée
1 dessertspoon paprika pepper
pinch of cayenne pepper
pinch of ground mace
salt
black pepper (ground from mill)
2 wineglasses red wine
1 wineglass stock, or water
1 tablespoon lemon juice (for poaching the fish)
bread (for croûtes)
oil (for frying)

This is a Basque fish dish and only those who really like garlic should make it.

Method

Heat the butter (or oil) in a shallow saucepan, add the onions and garlic, cover pan and allow them to soften slowly; then remove the lid and increase heat to brown them lightly. Add tomato purée and seasonings, mix well together, then add the wine and stock (or water). Bring sauce to the boil and simmer with the lid off for 10-15 minutes. Adjust seasoning and set sauce aside.

Set oven at 350°F or Mark 4. Wash, dry and trim the fish cutlets. Lay them in a buttered ovenproof dish and season; sprinkle with the lemon juice and poach in pre-set oven for 15-20 minutes. Cut a croûte of bread to fit each cutlet, fry them in oil until golden-brown on both sides. Arrange croûtes in a hot serving dish, set a fish cutlet on each one, then pour a good spoonful of the sauce over each. Serve very hot.

Note : a small quantity of thickening (kneaded butter or slaked arrowroot) can be added.

Cream of fish soup

$\frac{3}{4}$ lb fresh haddock fillet, or whiting
$1\frac{1}{2}$ oz butter
$1\frac{1}{2}$ oz plain flour
$\frac{1}{4}$ pint single cream
2 sprigs of parsley, or chervil

For stock
1 lb sole bones, or 1 turbot's head
1 large onion (peeled and sliced)
$\frac{1}{2}$ oz butter
1 carrot (sliced)
1 stick of celery (sliced)
2 pints water
bouquet garni
$\frac{1}{2}$ teaspoon salt
6 peppercorns
1 wineglass dry white wine
slice of lemon

Method

First prepare the stock. Wash the sole bones or turbot's head well, drain and set aside. Cover the onion with cold water, bring to the boil, drain and refresh. Melt $\frac{1}{2}$ oz butter in a large saucepan, put in the onion with the fish bones or head on top, cover and cook slowly for 5 minutes.

Add the sliced vegetables to the pan, pour over the water, add bouquet garni, seasoning, wine and lemon and simmer very gently for 20 minutes. Strain, measure $1\frac{3}{4}$ pints of the fish stock and set it aside.

Wash and dry the haddock or whiting, remove skin and then poach gently in the remaining fish stock. This can be done in a saucepan on top of the stove or in the oven, pre-set at 350°F or Mark 4, for about 10 minutes. Remove the bones and pound the fish to a fine purée.

Melt the $1\frac{1}{2}$ oz butter, stir in the flour off the heat and cook very gently to a pale straw colour. Blend in the reserved stock and stir until boiling, then simmer for 5-10 minutes. Whisk in the cream and fish purée ; taste for seasoning.

Break the parsley or chervil into sprigs and blanch, then add to the soup.

Serve the soup with fried croûtons.

Lotte in mayonnaise

2 lb white fish
2 pints court bouillon (see page 20)
3 thick slices of bread
2 tablespoons water
5 tablespoons olive oil
about $\frac{1}{2}$ clove of garlic (crushed
    with $\frac{1}{2}$ teaspoon salt)
a good squeeze of lemon juice
salt and pepper
$\frac{3}{4}$-1 pint mayonnaise
capers and sliced gherkins (to
    garnish)

If you cannot obtain lotte (angler) choose any thick-fleshed white fish such as rock salmon, cod, turbot or fresh tunny fish.

Method

Poach the fish in the court bouillon, with plenty of vegetables and herbs to flavour. Leave fish to cool in the liquor ; drain, bone and skin.

Soak the bread in the water and 1 tablespoon of the oil (add more liquid if this is not enough to soak it well), then squeeze as dry as possible. Crush the fish and work it well with the bread, then gradually add 3-4 tablespoons oil, the garlic and lemon juice. Season and finish with 2-3 tablespoons mayonnaise.

When of a creamy, but firm consistency, mound in a serving dish and coat with the remaining mayonnaise. Decorate with capers and sliced gherkins.

Fish crumble

$1\frac{1}{2}$ lb cooked white fish (cod,
    haddock, etc.) — flaked
3 hard-boiled eggs (roughly
    chopped)
4 oz prawns (optional)

For crumble mixture
$1\frac{1}{2}$ oz butter
3 oz plain flour
2 oz cheese (grated)
salt and pepper

For béchamel sauce
1 pint flavoured milk
$\frac{1}{2}$ oz plain flour
$\frac{1}{2}$ oz butter

Method

Set oven at 350°F or Mark 4.

To make the crumble, rub the butter and flour together, then add remaining ingredients. Set this mixture aside.

Make the béchamel sauce, then mix the fish with the chopped eggs and whole prawns. Blend this mixture with the béchamel sauce, and turn into an ovenproof dish.

Cover mixture with crumble topping and put in pre-set moderate oven for about 20-30 minutes to brown.

White fish flan

For rich shortcrust pastry
6 oz plain flour
3 oz butter
1 oz shortening
1 egg yolk
1-2 tablespoons water

For filling
1 cup white fish (cooked, flaked)
1 oz butter
1 cup finely sliced onions
1 rounded dessertspoon plain flour
$\frac{1}{4}$ pint milk
salt and pepper
grated nutmeg
2 eggs (beaten)
3 tomatoes (halved)
grated cheese

7-inch diameter plain or fluted flan ring

Method
Make up the rich shortcrust pastry and set aside to chill.

Line pastry on to the flan ring and bake blind. Set aside to cool. Turn oven setting to 375°F or Mark 5.

Heat butter in a pan, add onions and soften ; then mix in flour and add milk. Stir until boiling, draw pan aside, add seasoning and a dust of grated nutmeg, together with the beaten eggs.

Scald tomatoes, skin and flick out seeds, then cut in halves. Arrange tomatoes, cut side down, with white fish on bottom of flan, season well and pour over sauce. Scatter grated cheese on top and bake in pre-set oven for about 20-25 minutes until well set and golden-brown.

Fish Monte Carlo

1 lb white fish, or smoked haddock (cooked)
1 can sweetcorn kernels
1 oz butter
1 oz plain flour
$\frac{1}{2}$ pint milk
salt and pepper
pinch of mustard
2 eggs (separated)
2 oz cheese (grated)

For serving
4-5 bacon rashers
tomato sauce

Pie dish (1-1$\frac{1}{2}$ pints capacity)

Method
Remove the skin and bone from the fish and flake the flesh.

Drain sweetcorn, melt butter, add flour and mix. Pour on the milk, stir until boiling, season and add the mustard ; draw the pan aside and stir in the corn. Beat in the egg yolks and cheese, reserving a little for the top. Whip egg whites and fold into the sauce.

Butter an ovenproof dish, fill by layering the sauce and fish together, finishing with the sauce. Sprinkle with the remaining cheese and crumbs and bake in pre-set oven for 20-30 minutes.

Meanwhile grill the bacon. Garnish with the grilled bacon, and serve tomato sauce separately.

Oily fish

Oily fish are not as digestible as white fish, as the oil is distributed throughout the flesh instead of collected in the liver — but the rich flavour that results means that sauces and garnishes need to be of the simplest. Cold poached salmon with mayonnaise is a treat for a summer party, and grilled herring or mackerel will give you the tastiest meal you can think of — at a reasonable price.

Herrings

These are of the same family as sprats, whitebait, sardines and pilchards, and are perhaps the most widely known. They are a little smaller than mackerel and must be eaten very fresh.

Herrings can be grilled, rolled in oatmeal (whole or filleted) and fried, or soused in vinegar. They can also be cured, salted and smoked to become bloaters, kippers and buckling.

Sprats, whitebait and fresh sardines are fried ; pilchards are treated in the same way as herrings.

Heat oil or fat to 350°F or 370°F in deep fat bath. Put just enough whitebait into frying basket to cover bottom, lower into fat and fry for 2-3 minutes only.

Lift out, drain and tip on to absorbent paper. Repeat until all whitebait are fried. Then reheat fat to 400°F, oil to 375°F, put all fish into frying basket and fry until just brown and crisp (3-4 minutes). Drain, sprinkle with salt and pepper, or cayenne pepper. Serve hot.

Sprats

These are very like herrings but much smaller, and the fry (young) is often sold as whitebait. Smoked sprats are used in an hors d'oeuvre.

To fry sprats : first wash and dry in absorbent paper. Roll in seasoned flour, then fry in shallow or deep fat.

Whitebait

These tiny silvery fish are the fry of herring and are held in great esteem. Always deep fat fried, they are served as a first course with quarters of lemon and thinly-sliced brown bread and butter. They should be crisp yet slightly soft inside, and eaten heads, tail and all.

To fry whitebait (allow 4 oz per person) : spread out fish and pick over, discarding any broken ones or weed, but do **not** wash. Roll them in seasoned flour, shake in a bowl strainer to remove surplus flour (or put them in a paper bag containing some of the flour, shake well and tip out on to a strainer).

Herrings calaisienne

4 fresh herrings (with soft roes)
1 oz butter
1 tablespoon finely chopped onion
1 dessertspoon chopped parsley
  and thyme
2 eggs (hard-boiled and chopped)
1 clove of garlic (crushed with
  $\frac{1}{2}$ teaspoon salt)
pepper
1 thick slice of bread (soaked in a
  little milk)
grated rind of $\frac{1}{2}$ lemon
$\frac{1}{2}$ pint mustard sauce

Method

Cut heads from herrings, split down backs, remove backbones and roes. Wash and dry well. Set oven at 350°F or Mark 4.

Melt $\frac{1}{2}$ oz butter in a small pan, add onion and cook slowly until soft.

Meanwhile chop fish roes and place in a basin with herbs, chopped hard-boiled eggs, garlic and pepper. Squeeze liquid from the bread, chop and add to mixture with onion and lemon rind. Mix well to bind.

Put this mixture into the herrings, reshape and place in an ovenproof dish ; spread with remaining butter, cover with a piece of buttered paper and cook in pre-set oven for about 25 minutes or until fish is tender.

Pour mustard sauce on to serving dish and arrange the herrings on top.

A sharp mustard sauce is served with these baked stuffed herrings

Soused herrings

6 herrings (split and boned) —
2 extra for second helpings
salt and pepper
1 tablespoon pickling spice
1 bayleaf
1 onion (thinly sliced)
¾ pint vinegar and water (in equal proportions)

Method
Have herrings split and boned. Season cut surface and roll up from head to tail. Pack them in a deep dish or casserole. Set oven at 325°F or Mark 3.

Put pickling spice and bay-leaf into a pan with onion, vinegar and water. Add salt and bring to the boil. Cool, then pour over the herrings. The liquid should just cover them. Cook in the pre-set oven for about 1 hour. Serve the herrings cold.

Pickling spice is a selection of whole spices (pepper-corns, allspice and mace, etc.) and is a convenient way of buying spices if you do not use them frequently. If not using pickling spice for soused herrings, you will need 6 peppercorns, 2 blades of mace, 2 allspice berries and 1 clove. For a milder flavoured souse, add 1 tablespoon brown sugar to the vinegar and water. White wine can replace vinegar if preferred.

Smoked buckling
with mustard cream

4 smoked buckling

For cream sauce
4 tablespoons soured cream
1 teaspoon lemon juice
dash of French mustard
salt and sugar (to taste)

This can also be made with smoked trout, but use 2 tea-spoons grated horseradish instead of French mustard.

Method
Mix all the ingredients for the cream sauce and serve it in a sauce boat. Skin the buckling for serving and accompany with rye bread and butter. Serve as a first course.

Chopped herring

2 salt herrings
1 slice of bread
1 onion
1 large cooking apple
2 teaspoons caster sugar
pepper
2 hard-boiled eggs

Method
To prepare the herrings for use (if not bought ready-prepared): soak overnight to remove the salt, then skin and fillet.

Put the bread to soak in a little water and squeeze out well. Mince all the ingredients, reserving one egg yolk. Sieve the reserved yolk. Place the minced mixture on a serving dish ; sprinkle on the sieved yolk. Serve as a first course.

Stargazy pie

8 pilchards, or 6 herrings
8 oz quantity shortcrust pastry
1 small onion (finely chopped)
2 hard-boiled eggs (chopped)
1 tablespoon chopped parsley
1 teaspoon chopped herbs
salt and pepper
egg wash

9½-inch diameter pie plate

A speciality of Cornwall, this is really a pilchard or herring plate pie and can be very good if well made. Traditionally the heads of the fish are left on and stick out of the pie in the centre, hence the name 'stargazy'. This last touch has been known to put people off, so for the squeamish it can of course be omitted. The pie itself is good, cheap and nourishing.

Method
Set oven at 400°F or Mark 6. Bone out the fish, leaving on the heads. Roll out about half the pastry thinly and line the pie plate with it. Arrange the pilchards on top, with the heads in the centre. Scatter over chopped onion and eggs and the herbs ; season well. Roll out remaining pastry, cover the pie with this, press round the edge and trim off. Make a hole in the centre and draw the heads through this. Pinch round the outside edge of the pastry to decorate, and brush with egg wash. Bake in the pre-set oven, setting the plate on a hot baking sheet, for 15-20 minutes. When the pastry is a good brown colour, lower heat to 350-375°F or Mark 4-5 and continue cooking for a further 10 minutes, ie. 25-30 minutes in all.

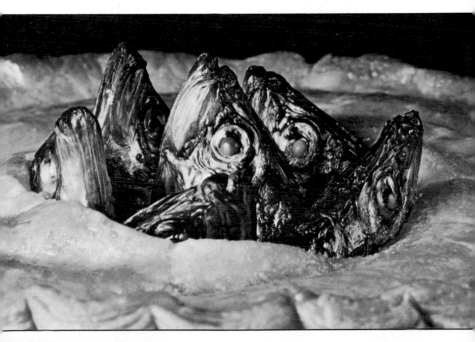

Herring pâté

3 buckling (smoked herrings)
salt
pepper (ground from mill)
juice of $\frac{1}{2}$ lemon
2 tablespoons white wine
$\frac{1}{2}$ lb fresh cod, or haddock, fillet
8 tablespoons fresh white bread-
$\frac{1}{2}$ crumbs
1 egg yolk
1 oz butter (melted)
1-2 tablespoons double cream
1 bayleaf

1-2 small terrines (oval ovenproof dishes with lids)

Method

Remove the skin and bones from the buckling and cut the flesh of two of them into finger-length pieces. Sprinkle with salt and pepper, pour over the lemon juice and wine and leave in this marinade for about 2 hours. Turn from time to time. Set oven at 325°F or Mark 3.

Meanwhile mince or pound the white fish with the remaining buckling and add the bread-crumbs, egg yolk, butter and cream. Stir in strained marinade and season to taste. Cover the bottom of the terrines with a layer of this mixture, then a layer of buckling pieces and repeat until all the ingredients are used, finishing with the white fish mixture. Put $\frac{1}{2}$ bayleaf on top of each terrine, cover with foil, put on the lids and bake au bain-marie in pre-set oven for about 45 minutes.

Remove lids, foil and bayleaf, leave pâté to cool, then cover with greaseproof paper and put a 1 lb weight on top of each one ; leave overnight. Pour a little extra melted butter on the tops and leave to set. Serve as a first course with freshly made toast and pats of unsalted butter.

Blending buckling and white fish with crumbs and egg mixture

Layering the marinated buckling pieces on to the pâté

Devilled herring roes

$\frac{1}{2}$ lb soft herring roes
1 tablespoon seasoned flour
clarified butter (for frying)
4 slices of bread (for toast)
2 oz anchovy butter
1 oz butter
squeeze of lemon juice
point of cayenne pepper, or a dash
  of Tabasco sauce
paprika pepper

Method
Wash the herring roes, put them in a colander and pour over a jug of boiling water, drain well. When cool, roll them in seasoned flour and fry in the clarified butter until brown and crisp. Wipe out the pan with absorbent kitchen paper and keep on one side.

Make the toast, trimming away the crusts, spread with the anchovy butter and cut in half ; arrange the herring roes on the pieces of toast and place on a hot dish.

Drop the 1 oz butter in the pan, heat until nut-brown, then add the lemon juice and cayenne or Tabasco, and while this mixture is foaming pour it over the roes. Dust with paprika and serve very hot.

Herring and dill cucumber salad

2-3 herring fillets
1 Spanish onion (sliced)
2 dill cucumbers (sliced)
French dressing (made with dry
   white wine instead of vinegar)

In many delicatessens herring
fillets preserved in white wine
may be bought quite cheaply.
These, cut into strips diagonally
and sprinkled with grated horseradish or mixed with horseradish cream, make an excellent
hors d'oeuvre. Alternatively,
these fillets may be made into a
salad as in this recipe. They
weigh about 4 oz each and are
sold by the fillet rather than by
the weight.

Method
Cut fillets into strips diagonally.
Set aside. Push onion slices out
into rings. Blanch for 5-6
minutes, then drain and refresh.
Arrange herring fillets in
centre of serving dish, surround
with the cucumber and place
the onion round that. Spoon
over enough French dressing
to moisten well.

*Herring and dill cucumber salad,
with onion rings and French dressing*

Hollandaise salad

3-4 fillets of smoked herring
    (according to size), or herring
    preserved in white wine
½ lb long grain Patna rice
1 tablespoon oil
2 dessert apples

For dressing
1 tablespoon mixed mustard
1 tablespoon vinegar
3-4 tablespoons olive oil
salt
pepper (ground from mill)

Method
If using smoked herring, soak in milk for about 1 hour to plump up the fillets. Dry these on absorbent paper and trim them into diagonal strips.

To prepare the dressing : combine the ingredients and season well. Put the pieces of herring in a dish and spoon over half the dressing.

Then boil the rice in plenty of salted water with the oil. After about 12 minutes, when it is just tender, drain, rinse with a little hot water and drain again. Spread the rice on a baking sheet and leave in an airy place to dry. When quite dry but still tepid, turn into a bowl and moisten with some dressing.

Pile up the pieces of herring (without their dressing) in the bowl with the rice. Quarter and core the apples (do not peel). Slice and arrange them over the rice. Spoon all remaining dressing over the apples. Chill this salad before serving.

Rollmop salad

6 rollmop herrings
4 medium-size potatoes
3-4 tablespoons French dressing
2 dill cucumbers
chopped parsley

Method
Scrub and cook potatoes in their skins until tender, drain and peel ; while still hot, slice and mix with some French dressing. Leave to cool. Put in the bottom of a salad bowl, then slice the cucumbers and cut the herrings into short strips ; mix them with the remaining dressing and arrange on top of the potatoes. Sprinkle well with chopped parsley.

Kipper fillets with lemon

2 cans (7 oz each) kipper fillets
  — drained
1 large onion (cut into rings)
1 bayleaf
lemon quarters

For marinade
1 teaspoon caster sugar
3 tablespoons white wine vinegar
4 tablespoons olive oil
salt and pepper (to taste)

This quantity gives 6-8 servings.

Method
Place kipper fillets in a shallow dish and cover with the onion rings and bayleaf. Mix together the ingredients for the marinade, pour it over the fillets and leave them to marinate for several hours.

Dish up fillets, individually, on lettuce leaves with quarters of lemon and slices of brown bread and butter. Serve as a first course.

Kipper pâté

3-4 kippers (according to size)
8 oz cream cheese
good pinch of paprika pepper
pepper (ground from mill)
salt (optional)
1-2 tablespoons single cream, or
  creamy milk

Method
Poach the kippers in water for 5-6 minutes and cool slightly in the liquid, then remove the skin and bones. Weigh the flesh — it should weigh 12 oz.

Work the cheese to a smooth cream, adding the paprika and pepper and, if necessary, a little salt. Add the cream (or creamy milk). Pound the kipper flesh, then gradually work it into the cheese. (This could be done by an electric mixer.) Adjust the seasoning and when pâté is soft and light pile it into a dish. Serve with devilled water biscuits (see below).

Devilled water biscuits

small water biscuits
melted butter
cayenne, or Nepal, pepper

Method
Brush biscuits with melted butter, sprinkle with the pepper and heat until piping hot in the oven (4-5 minutes).

Kipper kedgeree

1 packet of frozen kipper fillets
1 oz unsalted butter
2 oz long grain rice (cooked)
1 egg
2 tablespoons single cream
pepper (ground from mill)

Method

Cook kippers in their bag according to the instructions, and then flake them with a fork. Heat butter in a saucepan, add the cooked rice and the hot, flaked kipper fillets ; mix lightly with a fork.

Beat the egg with the cream, tip this on to the kipper mixture, season with pepper and continue stirring with a fork until the mixture is warmed through and the egg creamy.

Watchpoint Remember that eggs are quickly overcooked. Remove pan from heat while mixture is still a little liquid ; it will be quite set by the time you are ready to eat it.

Sardine relish

2 cans (4 oz each) sardines
salt and pepper
2-3 tablespoons olive oil
3 tablespoons chopped mixed
  herbs (including parsley)
3 tablespoons chopped capers
  or gherkins
1-1$\frac{1}{2}$ lb tomatoes
browned breadcrumbs, or a
  little grated cheese

Method

Set oven at 350°F or Mark 4.

Open cans of sardines and drain away the oil. Skin and bone the sardines, if preferred. Lay them in the bottom of a pie dish or gratin dish, season and sprinkle with a little of the oil.

Scatter over the herbs and capers (or gherkins). Scald and skin the tomatoes and cut into thick slices. Lay these in the pie dish to fill it. Sprinkle over the remaining oil and scatter with the crumbs or, if preferred, grated cheese. Bake in pre-set oven for 20-30 minutes.

Note : this dish is good served either hot or cold and may be done with tunny fish in place of sardines. It makes a good lunch or supper dish. If served cold, omit the crumbs.

Sardine and egg savoury

1 small can (4 oz) sardines
4 eggs (hard-boiled)
salt and pepper
2-3 drops of vinegar, or lemon
  juice
2 tomatoes (halved)
4 dessertspoons salad cream

Method

Split each sardine, remove the centre bone and tail and mash flesh with a fork. Halve the eggs lengthways, scoop out the yolks, add them to the sardines and mix well together until smooth. Season, and add the vinegar (or lemon juice).

Fill the egg whites with this mixture, reshape the eggs and set each one on a tomato half. Coat with salad cream and serve with brown bread and butter.

Eels

These are caught in fresh or salt water and are more often bought ready-cooked as jellied eels or eel pies. The flesh is rich with a delicate flavour and when smoked makes an excellent hors d'oeuvre.

Eels must be skinned before cooking ; ask your fishmonger to do this.

Stewed eels

2 lb eels (skinned)
1 onion (finely chopped)
salt and pepper
kneaded butter (made with 1 oz
  butter worked with $\frac{1}{2}$ oz plain flour)
squeeze of lemon juice
2 tablespoons chopped parsley

Method

Wash eels thoroughly and cut into 2-3 inch pieces. Put in a pan and just cover with cold water. Add onion and a little salt, cover and simmer for 20-30 minutes. Draw aside, add more salt, if necessary, and season well with pepper.

Add kneaded butter in small pieces. When dissolved, bring slowly to the boil, shaking pan gently. When boiling, add a good squeeze of lemon juice and parsley. Liquid should have the consistency of gravy and be plentiful. Serve in soup plates.

Jellied eels

2 lb eels
salt
2-3 tablespoons white wine
    vinegar, or juice of $\frac{1}{2}$ lemon
bouquet garni
6 white peppercorns
1 small onion (quartered)
gelatine (see method)
2 eggs (hard-boiled)
1 tablespoon sprigged, or
    coarsely chopped, parsley

*Plain 8-inch diameter cake tin, or
charlotte tin (1$\frac{1}{4}$ pints capacity)*

Method
Clean and skin the eels and cut
into 7-inch lengths. Place them
in a pan with warm water to
cover (about 1 pint). Season with
salt and vinegar (or lemon juce),
add the bouquet garni, peppercorns and onion. Simmer very
gently until the eels are tender
(about 30 minutes), then lift the
pieces from the pan with a
draining spoon and remove the
bones.

Strain the liquid, then return
it to the pan and bring it to the
boil ; skim very well. When the
liquid looks clear, measure it
and add gelatine in the pro-
portion of $\frac{1}{4}$ oz to every $\frac{1}{2}$ pint
liquid and stir carefully until it is
dissolved, strain again and cool.

Slice the hard-boiled eggs
and arrange slices in the tin,
then fill with the eel. Add the
parsley to the cold jelly and then
pour it very slowly and carefully
into the tin. Cover with foil and
leave in a cool place to set.
Turn out and serve with brown
bread and butter.

A green salad can accompany
the jellied eels and mayonnaise
may be served separately.

Spitchcocked eels

1 good-size eel, or 2 medium ones
seasoned flour
2 oz butter
2 tablespoons chopped parsley
1 tablespoon chopped thyme and
    sage (mixed)
1 small shallot (chopped)
salt and pepper
2 egg yolks
dry white breadcrumbs
4-5 tablespoons oil and 1 oz
    butter (for frying)
fried parsley (to garnish)

For sauce
1-2 oz butter
6 anchovies (pounded), or 1
    tablespoon anchovy essence
pepper

Method
Cut the prepared eel into 2-3
inch pieces and roll these in
seasoned flour. Melt the 2 oz
butter in a pan, add the herbs
and shallot and cook for 1
minute. Draw pan aside and
season. Roll the pieces of eel
in this mixture, then in egg and
breadcrumbs. Heat about 4-5
tablespoons oil in a deep
frying pan. Drop in 1 oz butter
and, while still foaming, put
in the pieces of eel. Fry gently
until golden-brown all over ;
lift out, drain well and dish up.
Keep eels hot while preparing
sauce.

Strain off any remaining fat
and wipe out the pan. Reheat
the pan, drop in the butter and,
when melted, add the anchovies
or essence ; swirl the pan round
gently to mix them thoroughly,
season well with pepper and
pour sauce over the eels.
Garnish with fried parsley.

Salmon

These are fish from 3 years old, weighing from 8 lb, an average weight being 12-16 lb. Under that age they are known as 'grilse' and weigh about 5-6 lb.

The season is from February to August but varies slightly according to area, some rivers having an earlier season than others. As salmon is an expensive fish, buy it when it is most plentiful, ie. from May to the end of July.

Whole fish cost slightly less per lb than fish bought by the piece, and they are suitable for a large party. A salmon is usually served cold, poached, skinned and suitably decorated. Allow 4-6 oz per person but take the head into account (it is about one-fifth of the total weight). Where possible, choose a fish with a small head and broad shoulders.

When buying in portions, the fish is scaled, but for cooking whole it is better left unscaled. This gives protection and makes it easier to skin when cooked.

The fishmonger will clean the salmon for you but, if you are doing it yourself, take care to remove the gills as well as the insides. Run your thumb down the backbone to remove the dark membrane which lies against it. Wash the salmon under cold running water and dry thoroughly before cooking. With scissors, snip away the fins and trim the tail into a 'vandyke' (ie. follow the line of the tail, and trim the centre of tail to a sharp 'V'). Leave on head.

Smaller cuts or steaks taken from the centre of the fish can weigh from 1½ 0 lb. Individual portions, such as cutlets, weigh from 4-6 oz and are poached or grilled.

Poaching For cooking a whole salmon, especially if it is large, a fish kettle with a lift-out drainer grid is essential because the salmon must be covered with liquid to poach it properly. The grid enables you to remove the fish without it breaking.

A salmon should be cooked in a court bouillon. This can be simply salted water or have vegetables, vinegar or wine added to flavour it. Salted water is adequate for a whole fish, but for a steak or cutlets use a flavoured court bouillon.

A tepid court bouillon, which gives a better colour to fish, is usual for larger pieces, but with smaller cutlets you should use a hot one, which prevents too much seepage from the fish.

If cutlets are to be eaten cold, the flavour is improved by adding wine to the court bouillon. In this case leave fish to cool in the liquid.

To dish up, carefully lift fish out of kettle with the grid. Rest this for a few seconds on a piece of muslin to dry fish as much as possible. Then peel off skin and remove centre bone, if wished.

Serve with mayonnaise or hollandaise sauce, a cucumber salad (see page 83) and 'fish' potatoes.

Smaller fish, such as grilse or salmon trout, can be cooked in the oven at 350°F or Mark 4 in an ovenproof dish with a small quantity of liquid ; they must be basted frequently. Alternatively, wrap fish in foil.

Cooking times for salmon, grilse and salmon trout are as follows :

Whole fish (over 5 lb) : 8 ▶

Salmon continued

minutes per lb.
Whole fish, or middle cuts
(under 5 lb) : 10 minutes per lb.
Whole fish (under 2 lb) :
10-20 minutes per lb.
Cutlets : 12-15 minutes, according to thickness.
Steaming. For a thick steak
or large piece of salmon, first
season, then wrap fish in buttered foil. Cook in a steamer or
fish kettle, allowing 20 minutes
per lb. If serving cold, cool
fish before unwrapping.

Salmon, or sea, trout

This is very like salmon but
smaller with pale pink, delicate
flesh. A fish weighs $1\frac{1}{2}$-$3\frac{1}{2}$
lb and is cooked whole. Salmon
trout are in season from May to
July.
The simplest way to cook
them is by poaching. Curl them
slightly after washing and trimming and put them into an ovenproof dish or tin. Pour round a
little water, add salt and a good
squeeze of lemon juice and
cover with foil or greaseproof
paper. Cook in the oven at
350°F or Mark 4, basting
frequently. Cooking times as for
salmon (see above).
Leave on the head because
this gives a good indication of
when the fish is cooked — the
eyes become firm and white.

Salmon fish cakes

1 **can (7$\frac{1}{2}$ oz) salmon**
$\frac{3}{4}$ **lb potatoes (peeled)**
1 **oz butter**
1 **tablespoon top of milk**
    (optional)
seasoned flour
fat (for frying)

This does not have to be made
with the best quality salmon.

Method
Drain the salmon and remove
any black skin and bones. Mash
flesh with a fork in a bowl.
Boil potatoes until they are
soft, tip off the water and
return pan to heat and dry the
potatoes thoroughly over gentle
heat. Mash them with the
butter, then tip into the bowl of
salmon. Mix fish and potatoes
together with a wooden spoon,
adding the top of the milk if
mixture is too dry.
Shape fish mixture into flat
even-size cakes, using two
knives to give them a neat
appearance, then roll or dust
them with seasoned flour. Shallow fry the fish cakes in a little
hot fat until golden-brown on
each side. Serve at once.

Salmon tourtière

2 lb salmon steak
4 oz long grain rice (boiled)
4 hard-boiled eggs (chopped)
1 tablespoon chopped mixed herbs
salt and pepper
1 egg (beaten)
pinch of ground mace

For rich shortcrust pastry
12 oz plain flour
pinch of salt
3 oz butter
3 oz lard, or shortening
2 egg yolks
5-7 tablespoons water

*8-inch diameter cake tin with loose
bottom, or spring form mould*

Method
Prepare the pastry and chill. Skin and bone the salmon, keeping the fillets whole. Chop any trimmings and mix with the rice, hard-boiled eggs, herbs, seasoning and beaten egg.

Set the oven at 400°F or Mark 6. Roll out the pastry, line into the cake tin, put a layer of the rice mixture on the bottom and set the fillets on this. Season with salt and pepper and ground mace. Cover with the rest of the rice and a 'lid' of the pastry. Seal and trim the edges, brush with egg and decorate.

Bake tourtière in the pre-set oven for 20-30 minutes, then lower heat to 350°F or Mark 4 and continue cooking for another 15-20 minutes. Remove it from the oven and cool before turning out of the tin. Take out by pushing up the loose bottom of the tin ; avoid turning out if possible. Serve cold with cucumber salad.

Cucumber salad

1 cucumber (peeled)
1 teaspoon salt
French dressing
fresh chives, or dill, or fennel
(in season) — snipped

Method
Peel cucumber and slice thinly. Spread slices on a plate and sprinkle with salt. Place another plate on top (bottom down) and set a weight on it. Leave for about 30 minutes. Then tilt the plates, holding them firmly together, to drain off the liquid before sliding the cucumber on to the serving dish.

Wachpoint When cucumbers are young the tender skin may be left on, which makes them easier to digest. The salting treatment also renders them more digestible. Under-season the dressing when cucumber has been salted.

Make French dressing, adding a good pinch of sugar if wished. Pour enough dressing over the cucumber to moisten it, grind on a little more pepper and sprinkle with snipped herbs.

Salmon mousse

$\frac{3}{4}$ lb salmon steak
2 oz butter
2 tablespoons double cream
(lightly whipped)
1 tablespoon medium sherry
2 drops of carmine colouring
(optional)

For court bouillon
$\frac{3}{4}$ pint water
juice of $\frac{1}{4}$ lemon, or 1 wineglass
white wine
$\frac{1}{2}$ teaspoon salt
3 peppercorns
bouquet garni

For béchamel sauce
$\frac{3}{4}$ cup of milk
$\frac{1}{2}$ bayleaf
1 blade of mace
6 peppercorns
1 slice of onion
1 oz butter
1 oz plain flour
salt

To finish
$\frac{1}{2}$ pint aspic jelly (cool but still liquid)
$\frac{1}{4}$ cucumber (thinly sliced)

*6-inch diameter top (No. 2 size)
soufflé dish*

This is a very rich mousse and you serve about 1 tablespoon as a portion. A cucumber salad could be offered, too, or just Melba toast.

Method
First make the court bouillon (see method, page 20), then put the salmon in a large pan, cover it with the hot court bouillon, bring this to the boil, then reduce the heat. Cover the pan and cook salmon very gently for 15 minutes ; allow fish to cool in the liquid, then drain it on absorbent paper and remove all the skin and bone.

Watchpoint The court bouillon must just 'tremble' throughout the cooking time. If you want to cook the salmon in the oven, cover it with greaseproof paper and baste it frequently ; allow 30 minutes at 325°F or Mark 4 (settings aren't comparable for this).

Prepare béchamel sauce then turn on to a plate to cool. Cream the butter until soft and lightly whip the cream. Work the salmon in a bowl with a wooden spoon or the end of a rolling pin, or pound with a pestle in a mortar.

Watchpoint Pounding the salmon is important : this breaks down the fibres of the fish and it will then hold the sauce and butter without them curdling.

Add the cold béchamel sauce and butter to the salmon and taste for seasoning. Fold in the cream and sherry. Add the carmine if the salmon is a very pale colour.

Turn mousse into soufflé dish, smooth the top with a palette knife and set in a cool place for about 10 minutes to firm. Pour over a thin layer of aspic jelly and when set arrange the cucumber on top, dipping each slice first in liquid aspic. When this garnish is set in position fill dish to the top with the remaining aspic.

Salmon trout Angers

1½ lb salmon trout
2 wineglasses white wine
1 wineglass water (to make
    ½ pint liquid)
squeeze of lemon juice
salt and pepper
bouquet garni
1 shallot (chopped)
1 oz butter
3 egg yolks
3 tablespoons double cream
1½ oz unsalted butter
1 cucumber

Method

Trim, wash and dry the trout, place it in a shallow pan with the wine, water, lemon juice and seasonings. Cover pan and bring it very gently to simmering point, draw the pan to the side of the stove, cover and leave fish to poach for 20 minutes. Drain fish and reserve liquor.

Place shallot in a pan with about ½ oz butter and cook it slowly until golden, then tip on the fish liquor and allow it to reduce by half. Mix the egg yolks and cream, stir in 2 tablespoons of the hot liquid, then add this liaison to the pan to thicken sauce. Remove pan from the heat, beat in the unsalted butter a little at a time, and pass the sauce through a conical strainer, if necessary.

Peel cucumber and quarter it lengthways, then cut it across into small chunks. Cook in ½ oz butter in a covered frying pan for 7-8 minutes or until just tender. Season well.

Skin fish and carefully lift on to a hot serving dish ; strain any extra liquid left in the pan into the sauce. Spoon the sauce over the fish and serve hot with the cucumber arranged on either side of the fish.

Trout

A fresh-water fish, found in rivers, lakes and streams, with silvery brown skin and white flesh, although some trout may be pink-fleshed. They are in season from February to early September, but at their best from April to August.

Trout grenobloise

4-5 even-size trout
½ pint water
2 lemons
6 peppercorns
1 slice of onion
1 dessertspoon grated
    horseradish
2-3 tablespoons dry sherry
salt, pepper and sugar (to taste)
4 tablespoons single cream
chopped parsley

Method

Set oven at 350°F or Mark 4.

Clean and trim the trout. Place them in a casserole with the water, squeeze of lemon juice, peppercorns and onion and poach in pre-set oven for about 15 minutes.

Cool trout in the liquid, then take them up carefully and skin them. Arrange in the dish for serving.

Pare off a little of the lemon rind, cut into fine strips and blanch. Remove the white pith from the lemon and cut fruit into segments. Put the horseradish, sherry, salt, pepper and sugar into a bowl, mix in the cream carefully and add the lemon. Spoon this sauce over the trout and scatter on the lemon rind and chopped parsley. Serve with brown bread and butter.

Trout Belin

4-5 trout
seasoned flour
about 6 oz butter (for frying)
juice of 1 lemon and 1 orange
1 tablespoon chopped parsley

For farce
4 shallots
5 oz mushrooms (chopped)
3 large handfuls of spinach
   (blanched), or 1 packet of frozen
   leaf spinach — chopped with 1
   tablespoon mixed herbs
salt and pepper

For garnish
1 large orange
1 dessertspoon caster sugar
few sprigs of watercress

Method
Bone out the trout (see opposite) and set aside.

To prepare farce, finely chop the shallots, soften them in about 1-1$\frac{1}{2}$ oz butter, add the mushrooms and spinach and herbs. Season, cover pan and simmer for 5-6 minutes. Leave farce to cool, then fill into the trout. Reshape them and roll carefully in seasoned flour.

Fry stuffed trout in butter until brown on both sides, turning them once. Season with salt and ground pepper, dish up on a hot serving dish and keep warm.

Wipe out the pan, slice the orange into it and fry quickly in $\frac{1}{2}$ oz butter, dusting with a little caster sugar until it turns colour ; then take out orange and reserve.

Wipe out the pan, reheat and drop in about 2 oz butter. Cook until it is a nut-brown, then quickly add the lemon and orange juices and chopped parsley. Pour this at once over the trout and surround with the orange slices and garnish the dish with watercress.

Boning trout

First snip off the fins and vandyke the tail with scissors. Cut off the head and, with a sharp knife, slit down the back, keeping the knife on top of the backbone. Open up the fish until it lies flat on the working surface. Slip the knife under the bone at the head end and cut down to just above the tail. Lift out the bone.

Cutting head off raw trout before slitting down back to remove bone

Tunny fish

One of the mackerel family (sometimes known as 'tuna'), this is found in warm seas such as the Mediterranean and some parts of the Atlantic. The flesh is white, firm and meaty. The fresh fish may be grilled or boiled, but in Britain tunny is usually available only in cans, mostly prepared in oil.

Cream of tunny fish and egg

2 cans ($7\frac{1}{2}$ oz) tunny fish
4 hard-boiled eggs
1 tablespoon browned breadcrumbs and grated cheese
   (mixed together)

For sauce
2 oz onions (finely sliced)
$1\frac{1}{2}$ oz butter
$\frac{3}{4}$ oz plain flour
$\frac{1}{2}$- $\frac{3}{4}$ pint milk
salt and pepper
2 oz cheese (grated)

Pie dish (1-1$\frac{1}{2}$ pints capacity)

Method

First prepare the sauce. Soften onion in half the butter, add the remainder and stir in the flour off the heat. Pour on the milk, stir until boiling, season, then draw aside and beat in the cheese by degrees.

Pour a little sauce into an ovenproof dish, flake the tunny fish and arrange on top with the sliced or halved eggs. Coat with the rest of the sauce. Scatter with crumbs and cheese and brown in a quick oven, at 450°F or Mark 8, or under grill.

Tunny fish cream

10-12 oz canned tunny fish
2 eggs (separated)
$2\frac{1}{2}$ fl oz double cream
$\frac{1}{2}$-$\frac{3}{4}$ pint tomato sauce

For panade
2 oz butter
2 oz plain flour
1 rounded dessertspoon tomato
   purée
$\frac{1}{2}$ pint light stock, or milk, or water
salt and pepper

To fill mould
green peas, or new carrots

Ring mould (1$\frac{1}{2}$ pints capacity)

Method
Well flake the tunny fish, then crush it and work it with any oil from the can.

To prepare the panade : melt butter, stir in the flour with tomato purée, then blend in stock (or milk, or water) ; stir until boiling, season well and turn out to cool. When cold gradually beat panade into the fish mixture with egg yolks and cream ; whip whites to a stiff froth, then cut and fold them into the mixture. Turn cream into the well buttered mould, cover with foil or buttered paper and steam it, or poach au bain-marie, for 45-50 minutes or until firm to the touch. Leave cream for 5 minutes before turning out.

Have ready the tomato sauce and freshly cooked young peas. Alternatively cook young carrots whole but keep a small portion of the green tops on ; toss them in a little butter when drained. Turn out the cream. Coat with a little of the tomato sauce, fill the centre with the peas or carrots, or a mixture of both, and serve the rest separately.

Pacific pie

about 15 oz canned tunny fish
1 medium-size can condensed
   cream of chicken soup
1 small packet of frozen peas
3 medium-size tomatoes
   (skinned, seeds removed, and
   sliced)
1 large packet of potato crisps
2 tablespoons finely grated cheese

Method
First cook the peas (following instructions on packet).

Set the oven at 350°F or Mark 4. Drain and flake the tunny fish. Put a layer of the fish into an ovenproof casserole, with half of the soup, half of the peas, half of the tomatoes and half of the crisps. Repeat the layers, finishing with remaining crisps and grated cheese.

Put pie into pre-set oven for 30 minutes, then finish off by browning under grill before serving with either boiled rice or creamed potatoes.

For a supper dish, make this Pacific pie topped with crisps and cheese

Tunny fish salad

1 can (7½ oz) tunny fish
1 dessert apple
2 cooked potatoes (diced)
2 sticks of celery (diced)
1 small can (7½ oz) beetroot, or
   ½ jar small whole beetroots (diced)
1 small can (5 oz) peas, or small
   packet of frozen peas

For dressing
3 tablespoons salad cream
2 tablespoons double cream, or
   evaporated milk, or plain
   yoghourt
salt and pepper
sugar (to taste)
¼ clove of garlic (crushed) —
   optional

Method
Drain the tunny fish, put it into a bowl and flake with a fork.

Peel, core and dice apple. Add apple and potato to tunny fish.

To prepare the dressing : mix salad cream and cream (or evaporated milk or yoghourt) together, season with a little extra salt and pepper and sugar, and the garlic, if liked.

Pour the dressing over the mixture in the bowl and mix carefully with a fork. Turn salad into a serving dish and add the celery, beetroot and peas. Surround with lettuce hearts (or watercress) and tomato slices.

Tunny fish and egg salad

2 cans (7½ oz each) tunny fish
4 eggs (hard-boiled)
2 lb tomatoes
1½ cucumbers (peeled)
salt
1 lb frozen French, or sliced, beans
1 small can anchovy fillets
1 tablespoon mixed chopped herbs
(½ parsley, ¼ mint and ¼ chives)
French dressing (made from
   2 tablespoons white wine vinegar,
   salt and pepper, 6 tablespoons
   salad oil)
12 black olives (halved and stoned)

Large gratin dish

If no fresh herbs are available,
use ½ tablespoon dried basil
and oregano (mixed).

Method

Scald and skin the tomatoes;
cut ½ lb into quarters and the
remainder in thick slices. Slice
the half cucumber very finely,
salt it and keep between 2
plates. Cut the other cucumber
in thicker slices, or into small
cubes, and sprinkle with salt.
Cook the beans in boiling water
until tender and then drain and
refresh. Drain the anchovy fillets
from the oil and cut each fillet
in half lengthways.

Flake the tunny fish and slice
the hard-boiled eggs. Layer the
sliced tomatoes, beans and
thickly cut cucumber (drained
of the water), tunny fish and
hard-boiled eggs in a large
gratin dish. Add the herbs to
the French dressing, whisk well
and spoon over the salad.
Place the thinly cut cucumber,
also drained of water, over the
top of the salad. Arrange the
anchovy fillets in a lattice over
the top of the cucumber and
place a half olive in each
square. Arrange the quartered
tomatoes around the outside
of the dish.

Serve with potatoes baked in
their jackets.

Mackerel

This is a rich and delicious fish with firm flesh. At its best in late spring and summer, mackerel must be eaten as fresh as possible, otherwise the flesh is too oily and unpalatable.

Good mackerel average 1-1½ lb in weight and are best filleted before being cooked. Roll the well dried fillets in seasoned flour and fry in bacon fat or butter ; alternatively they can be grilled. Serve sizzling hot with quarters of lemon. This is one of the best ways to serve freshly caught mackerel.

If you find mackerel on the rich side, try poaching the fillets in the oven at 375°F or Mark 5 for 10-15 minutes in a little salted water with juice of ½ lemon added. Drain and serve with a good sprinkling of freshly chopped parsley accompanied by boiled or 'fish' potatoes.

Mackerel with Venetian sauce

2-3 mackerel (according to size)
— filleted
salt
squeeze of lemon juice

For sauce
¼-½ cucumber
handful of spinach
sprig of tarragon and chervil
2½ oz butter
1 dessertspoon plain flour
½ pint water
salt and pepper
2 egg yolks
2 shallots (finely chopped)

Method

Set oven at 350°F or Mark 4. Prepare mackerel fillets : lay the fish on a piece of wet, rough cloth (to prevent slipping) and, keeping the fish steady with one hand, take a thin sharp knife or filleting knife and first trim away the fins ; then remove the head and cut down the back with the blade on top of the backbone.

Lift off the top fillet. Now slip the knife under the bone at the top and keep it as close as possible to the backbone ; work down to the tail, using short sharp strokes.

Wash and dry the fillets, put them in an ovenproof dish. Barely cover with water, add salt and a good squeeze of lemon juice. Poach in the pre-set oven for 12-15 minutes.

Meanwhile prepare sauce : peel and dice cucumber ; blanch for 3 minutes in a pan of boiling water, then drain and set aside. Cook spinach and herbs in a pan of boiling salted water for about 5 minutes. Then drain, press out moisture and rub through a wire strainer, or mix in a blender.

Melt $\frac{1}{2}$ oz butter in a pan and stir in flour. Whisk in the water with seasoning ; bring to boiling point only and then draw aside ; beat in egg yolks and remaining butter, a small piece at a time. Add spinach and herb purée and adjust seasoning.

Take up the fish, put on a serving dish, pour the liquid off into a pan ; add shallots and boil until liquid is reduced to 3-4 tablespoons. Strain this into the sauce. Reheat sauce

gently but do not boil. Add cucumber and spoon sauce over the fillets. Serve hot.

Having trimmed away fins, removed the head and cut down the back of the mackerel so as to lift off top fillet, cut away the backbone with short, sharp strokes of the knife

Mackerel with mushrooms and tomatoes

2-3 mackerel (according to size)
— filleted
seasoned flour
4 tablespoons dripping, or oil
1 small onion (finely chopped)
$\frac{1}{4}$ lb flat mushrooms (chopped)
1 clove of garlic (chopped)
1 dessertspoon chopped mixed
herbs, or parsley
2 tablespoons wine vinegar
salt and pepper
$\frac{3}{4}$ lb tomatoes (skinned and sliced)

Method
Fillet fish as for previous recipe. Wash and dry fillets and then roll them in seasoned flour.

Heat the frying pan, put in 2 tablespoons dripping or oil. When hot, lay in the fillets, cut side downwards, and fry until a good brown ; then turn and cook on the other side.

Lift out fillets and put them on a serving dish, overlapping them ; keep warm in oven.

Wipe out the pan, reheat and add 1 tablespoon of dripping or oil. Put in the chopped onion and cook slowly to soften it ; then add the mushrooms and chopped garlic. Fry briskly for 2-3 minutes, then add herbs, vinegar and season to taste. Reboil and pour over the fish.

Sauté tomatoes in remaining dripping or oil for 1-2 minutes, then put round fish or at either end of the dish. Serve hot.

Lay fried mackerel fillets in the dish with the sliced tomatoes at each end and the mushroom and onion mixture down the centre

Shellfish

All shellfish make attractive and unusual additions to the table, either on their own or in a sauce with other fish. Whether fresh from British shores or imported, shellfish need careful preparation and must be eaten very fresh. But don't let the need for care deter you from preparing some of the delights on the following pages — your guests will think the trouble well worth while.

Crab

Crabs are in season in Britain from May to September and are usually sold ready cooked. If alive, boil them gently in salted water or a court bouillon (allow 15 minutes per lb). Then cool in the liquid before taking out and allowing to get quite cold. The crab is then dressed, whether it is to be served hot or cold. Some fishmongers sell them dressed or will dress them for you at a small extra charge.

Good crabs are heavy for their size. The claws contain most of the white meat, the cock's claws being larger than the hen s. Frozen crab meat, both white and brown, is available throughout the year, and is excellent for mousses and soufflés, both hot and cold and for savouries. For 4 people allow a 2 lb crab or 2 smaller ones.

To dress crab : first remove big claws, and set aside, then twist off the small claws, at the same time removing the crab's body or undershell. Set aside. Take out and throw away the following parts :

1 The small sac lying in the top of the big shell
2 Any green matter in the big shell
3 The spongy fingers or lungs lying around the big shell

Using a teaspoon, scrape into a small bowl all the brown creamy part lying round the sides of the big shell. Now take a cloth and, holding the big shell firmly, break down the sides, which are recognisably marked. The shell should now be well washed and dried.

Cut the body of the crab into two and extract all the white meat with a skewer and place in a bowl, but take care not to break off any fine pieces of shell. Crack the big claws, extract all the meat and shred it, break it up well, again avoiding breaking off any fine pieces of shell.

Collect all the white meat together ; thoroughly cream the brown part and season it well with pepper, salt and mustard. Add about 2 tablespoons of dry breadcrumbs (and 1 tablespoon of cream if the mixture seems stiff). This brown mixture is then arranged across the middle of the shell with the white meat piled on either side. When serving crab cold, you can decorate it with sieved, hard-boiled egg and some chopped parsley. Make a ring of claws by sticking the small ones into one another and lay the shell in the middle of this. Surround with crisp lettuce leaves, radishes, etc. and serve with mayonnaise, or tartare sauce, or a sharp French dressing, all with brown bread and butter. Alternatively serve with pats of maître d'hôtel butter and hot toast.

1 *For dressed crab remove claws*
2 *Take the lungs out of the crab*
3 *Break down sides of big shell*
4 *Put crab meat and egg in shell*
5 *Dressed crab, garnished with sieved boiled egg and chopped parsley, crab claws, lettuce, and radishes cut to form roses ; serve with a dressing such as mayonnaise or tartare sauce and brown bread and butter, or with maître d'hôtel butter and hot toast*

1

2

3

4

5

Crab and rice salad

4-5 oz canned crab claw meat
6 oz long grain rice
1 green, or red, pepper
1 clove of garlic (cut)
salt and pepper
3 oz black olives (stoned)
2 oz button mushrooms (thinly
   sliced)
1 oz walnut kernels (coarsely
   chopped)

For dressing
juice of 1 small lemon
3-4 tablespoons olive oil
salt
pepper (ground from mill)

Shredding red pepper for crab and rice salad, with sliced mushrooms and olives ready for mixing into salad

Method

Turn out the crab meat and flake with a fork. Boil the rice until tender (about 12 minutes), drain, rinse with a little hot water and drain again. Spread rice on a baking sheet and leave in an airy place to dry. Shred and blanch the pepper.

Combine the ingredients for the dressing. Rub the cut clove of garlic round the serving dish.

While the rice is still warm, season it well with salt and pepper and mix with the dressing. When quite cold, stir in the crab meat, shredded pepper, olives and raw mushrooms. Fork up well to mix thoroughly and scatter walnuts over the top.

Mixing the cold rice with the crab meat, red pepper, olives and mushrooms before adding walnuts

Crab flan

8 oz quantity of rich shortcrust
pastry

For filling
1 lb frozen crab meat ($\frac{1}{2}$ dark and
  $\frac{1}{2}$ white meat)
$\frac{1}{4}$ pint thick béchamel sauce
2 oz butter (creamed)
salt and pepper
1-2 tablespoons double cream
1 cucumber
black pepper (ground from mill)
$\frac{1}{4}$ pint mayonnaise
2 eggs (hard-boiled)

8-9 inch diameter flan ring

Method
First make the pastry, line it into
the flan ring and bake blind.
Set aside to cool.

Finely slice the cucumber,
sprinkle with salt between
slices and leave them pressed
between two plates for 30
minutes ; drain and rinse with
ice-cold water. Dry cucumber
and season with black pepper.

Work the cold béchamel
sauce into the dark crab meat,
add creamed butter, seasoning
and lightly whipped cream.

Mix the mayonnaise with the
white crab meat.

Put the dark crab meat and
cucumber in the flan case, then
the white crab meat. Shred
white of the eggs and mix with
chopped parsley, sieve yolks
and use both to decorate the
flan.

Crab ramekins

8 oz white crab meat
1 teaspoon tomato purée
1 glass sherry
1 can consommé (about 10$\frac{3}{4}$ fl oz)

8 ramekin dishes

Method
Mix the tomato purée with the
sherry and gently stir in the
consommé. Lift the crab meat
with a fork into the ramekin
dishes ; this is to make sure that
the crab meat does not get
tightly packed.

Spoon over the prepared consommé and put in refrigerator
for at least 1 hour to set.

Scalloped crab

1 large crab, or 1 large can crab
  claw meat
$\frac{3}{4}$ pint béchamel sauce
3-4 sticks celery (finely sliced)
salt and pepper
4 tablespoons breadcrumbs
2 tablespoons grated Cheddar
  cheese
1 oz butter

Method
Have the crab ready and
the béchamel sauce prepared.
Set oven at 350°F or Mark 4.

Mix the sliced celery with the
crab meat and sauce and
season to taste. Tip the mixture
into a buttered gratin dish, cover
with the breadcrumbs and
cheese, dot with the butter and
bake in the pre-set oven for 20
minutes or until hot, and brown
on top.

Crab soufflé

¾ lb crab meat (white and
   brown, or all white)
2 shallots (finely chopped)
1 oz butter
1 teaspoon each curry powder
   and paprika pepper
2 tablespoons single cream
1-2 tablespoons sherry
¼ pint béchamel sauce (made with
   1 oz butter, 1 tablespoon flour,
   ¼ pint flavoured milk)
dash of Tabasco sauce
salt and pepper
3 egg yolks
4 egg whites
browned breadcrumbs
grated Parmesan cheese

*6-inch diameter top (No. 2 size)
soufflé dish*

Method

Grease the soufflé dish and tie
a band of greaseproof paper
round it so that it extends 3
inches above top of dish. Grease
inside the paper rim. Set oven
at 375°F or Mark 5.

Soften shallots in half the
butter, add curry powder and
paprika and cook for 2 seconds.
Add to the crab meat with the
cream and sherry. Have ready
the béchamel sauce, beat it
into the crab meat with the
seasonings and egg yolks.
Whip whites to a firm snow,
then cut and fold them into the
mixture. Turn into prepared
dish, dust top with crumbs and
cheese. Bake in pre-set oven
for 20-30 minutes. Serve the
soufflé at once.

Devilled crab

1 large dressed crab (about 1½ lb)
1 small onion (finely chopped)
1½ oz butter
3 tablespoons white breadcrumbs
1 tablespoon grated dry cheese
2 tablespoons single cream
1 teaspoon anchovy essence
speck of mustard
pinch of cayenne pepper, or 2-3
   drops Tabasco sauce
dash of Worcestershire sauce

For browning
browned breadcrumbs
grated Parmesan cheese
extra melted butter

For serving
2 bananas (plus butter for frying)
lemon juice
devilled water biscuits

This makes a good lunch dish,
or a substantial savoury.

Method

Set oven at 400°F or Mark 6.
Turn crab meat into a mixing
bowl. Soften onion in pan in
half the butter, then add last
¾ oz ; when melted add this to
the crab with the white crumbs,
cheese, cream, anchovy essence,
seasoning and Worcestershire
sauce. When well spiced put
back into the shell, smooth top,
sprinkle with browned crumbs,
grated Parmesan cheese and
melted butter. Brown in the pre-
set oven for 10-15 minutes.

Meanwhile, peel each banana
and cut into three diagonal
slices. Fry quickly in hot butter,
sprinkle with a little cayenne
pepper and lemon juice. Arrange these on, or round, the
crab. Serve with devilled water
biscuits (see page 77).

Prawns

Prawns are usually sold ready boiled. Fresh prawns in season are best (the season being spring and summer), but the excellence of the frozen variety makes them an all-year-round delicacy. However, quick thawing toughens them and spoils the flavour, so they are best bought the day before and left overnight in the body of the refrigerator, or a very cool larder. They should then be succulent and tender.

To shell prawns bought by the dozen or the pint : start to peel the body shell away where it joins the head, then give the tail a firm pinch and draw it gently off the meat. Twist off the head. When used for garnish, the body and tail shell only is removed, the head being lightly rubbed with oil.

Dublin Bay prawns are the largest and best of the prawn family. If bought raw, in the shell, boil them gently in a court bouillon for 10-15 minutes. Serve them cold as a first course with mayonnaise or French dressing and brown bread and butter. The meat is sweet and delicious and is easier to get at if the body and claw shells are lightly cracked before serving, Have finger bowls on the table and a small fork or lobster pick for each guest.

Scampi are very large Adriatic prawns. Frozen scampi must be allowed to thaw out gradually (12 hours or more in a refrigerator). If using fresh Dublin Bay prawns in a scampi recipe, remove head and claws and cut away the body shell after cooking.

Prawn bouchées

8 oz quantity of puff pastry
egg wash (made with 1 egg beaten with $\frac{1}{2}$ teaspoon salt)

For filling
4-6 oz prawns (shelled and chopped)
1$\frac{1}{2}$ oz butter
1 rounded tablespoon plain flour
$\frac{1}{2}$ pint milk (infused with 1 slice of onion, $\frac{1}{2}$ bayleaf, 6 peppercorns)
salt and pepper

2$\frac{1}{2}$-inch diameter fluted cutter, 1$\frac{1}{2}$-inch diameter cutter (fluted, or plain)

Method

Set oven at 425°F or Mark 7. Roll out pastry to just over $\frac{1}{4}$ inch thick and stamp it out into bouchées 2$\frac{1}{2}$inches in diameter. Set on a dampened baking sheet and brush with egg wash. Make circular incisions with the smaller cutter to form lids. Bake in pre-set oven for 15-20 minutes until golden-brown.

Make a white sauce, season and stir in the prawns.

Remove lids and fill bouchées with the mixture. Replace lids and reheat a few minutes in oven before serving very hot.

If you have baked bouchées a few days before, the best way to reheat them is as follows : first set oven at 350°F or Mark 4. Fill cold bouchées with hot filling and heat for 10 minutes.

Prawns sicilienne

6 oz long grain rice (boiled)
French dressing (to moisten)
paprika pepper
1½ oz almonds (blanched and
  shredded)
salt and pepper

For sauce
¼ pint thick mayonnaise
juice of 1 orange
juice of ½ lemon
1-2 caps of pimiento (sieved)
1 shallot (finely chopped)
2¼ fl oz strong fresh tomato
  pulp (see page 50)
4 oz prawns (shelled)

6-8 dariole moulds

Method
Mix the rice with French dressing (coloured with the paprika)
and add the almonds. Season
well. Put into the dariole moulds
and set aside.
  To prepare the sauce : combine the ingredients in the order
given, and adjust seasoning.
Turn out the moulds and spoon
the sauce round the rice.
Watchpoint Soak almonds
(either before or after splitting
and shredding) in warm water
for 30 minutes or longer. This
makes them juicy and tender
and like a fresh nut. Drain well
and dry before adding to rice.

Prawn curry

1 lb shelled prawns
1 tablespoon pounded coriander
  seeds
1 teaspoon cumin powder
about 1 teaspoon chilli powder
  (to taste)
½ teaspoon ground turmeric
1 clove of garlic (crushed with salt)
1 large onion (finely sliced)
2 tablespoons oil
salt
2 tomatoes (skinned and chopped)
1 dessertspoon coconut cream
  (softened in 2 tablespoons warm
  water)
½ pint fish stock, or water
pinch of sugar
juice of ½ lemon

Method
Mix the spices and the garlic
to a paste with a little water.
Fry the onion in the oil until
brown. Add the paste and cook
for 1-2 minutes, adding a tablespoon of water, if necessary, to
prevent sticking. Add all the
ingredients, except prawns and
lemon juice. Simmer gently until
sauce is thick (about 20 minutes), then put in the prawns
and lemon juice. Cook for a
further 5 minutes. Serve with
boiled rice and any other accom-
paniment you want.

Prawn and egg mousse

8 oz prawns (frozen, or fresh) —
   peeled and very finely chopped
12 eggs (hard-boiled and peeled)
¾ pint mayonnaise
2 egg whites
1½ oz gelatine
¼ pint stock, or wine, or water
salt and pepper

For béchamel sauce
2 oz butter
2 oz plain flour
1 pint milk (flavoured with 1 teaspoon paprika pepper and 1 teaspoon tomato purée)

For devilled garnish
1 lb tomatoes
8 oz prawns (frozen, or fresh)
   — peeled
2-3 drops of Tabasco sauce
1 teaspoon tomato ketchup
3 tablespoons French dressing

small cress, or cucumber, or watercress and extra slices of tomato

Ring mould (2¼ pints capacity)

Method

First oil the mould, then divide the hard-boiled eggs in half, remove the yolks and rub them through a wire strainer ; chop the egg whites.

Prepare the béchamel sauce and, when cold, pound with the prawns and sieved egg yolks until smooth, then work in the mayonnaise.

Stiffly whip the egg whites ; dissolve the gelatine in the stock (or wine or water) and add to the mayonnaise mixture with the chopped egg whites and season well: As the mixture begins to thicken, fold in the egg whites. Turn mousse into the oiled mould and leave to set (about 2 hours).

Prepare the garnish. Scald and skin the tomatoes and cut them into four. Remove the hard core and the seeds, then cut the flesh into fine shreds. Add the Tabasco sauce and tomato ketchup to the French dressing and mix this with the tomatoes and prawns.

When the mousse is set, turn it out on a large dish and fill the centre with the devilled tomatoes and prawns. Garnish the dish with a salad of your choice : small cress, cucumber, watercress and extra slices of tomato.

Garnishing prawn and egg mousse with sliced tomatoes and watercress

Prawns Frederick

1 lb prawns (shelled)
1 small head of celery (cut in
   small sticks)
little cornflour
oil (for frying)
6 oz long grain rice (boiled)
3 quarts salted water

For sauce
2 onions
3 tablespoons oil
1 teaspoon curry powder
7½ fl oz tomato juice, or tomato
   cocktail
1 dessertspoon tomato purée
salt and pepper
2-3 tablespoons tomato and pepper
   chutney, or a sweet tomato
   chutney, or pickle

The sauce, which is best made
well before frying the prawns so
that it can mellow, is also good
with fried or grilled fish.

Method

To prepare sauce : slice onions,
cook in hot oil until turning
colour, add curry powder and,
after 1-2 minutes, tip on the
tomato juice. Add tomato purée,
season to taste, and simmer for
5 minutes. Draw aside and add
the chutney.

Cut celery in small sticks,
roll these and the prawns in
cornflour, fry at once in a pan of
hot oil to a golden-brown.

Pour over the sauce and serve
at once with boiled rice.

Prawn flan

For rich shortcrust pastry
8 oz plain flour
4 oz butter
2 oz shortening
1 egg yolk
2 tablespoons water (to mix)

For filling
8 oz shelled prawns
4 eggs (hard-boiled)
¼ pint mayonnaise
1 small cucumber
black pepper
1 tablespoon chopped dill, or
   chives
6 anchovy fillets
2-3 tablespoons milk

8-9 inch diameter flan ring

Method

Prepare the pastry and set
aside to chill for about 30
minutes. Roll it out and line
into the flan ring and bake blind
for about 15 minutes.

Meanwhile prepare the filling.
Cut the cucumber into small
dice, sprinkle lightly with salt
and cover ; keep in a cool place
for 30 minutes, then drain,
season with black pepper and
add the herbs. Shred the egg
whites and mix with the prawns
and mayonnaise. Sieve the egg
yolks, cover and set aside.
Divide the anchovy fillets in
half lengthways and soak in the
milk to remove the excess salt.

When the pastry case is cool,
fill with the prawn mixture and
arrange a thick border of
cucumber around the edge. Fill
the centre with sieved egg yolk
and cover with a lattice of
anchovy fillets. Serve cold.

Chilled prawn bisque

6 oz shelled prawns (chopped)
1 onion (finely chopped)
1 oz butter
2 lb tomatoes, or 1 can (1 lb 14 oz) tomatoes
3 caps of canned pimiento (chopped)
1 dessertspoon tomato purée
2-2½ pints chicken stock
little arrowroot (mixed with water)
¼ pint double cream

This soup can also be served hot.

Method
Cook the onion in the butter until softened, then add the tomatoes (skinned, cut in half and squeezed to remove the seeds). Cover the pan and slowly cook the vegetables to a pulp. Add the pimiento, tomato purée and stock. Simmer for 10-15 minutes. Then add the prawns and work in an electric blender. Thicken the soup lightly with the slaked arrowroot and chill.
Note : if a blender is not used, pass the vegetables and liquid through a fine sieve and add the prawns, finely chopped, after the soup has been thickened.
Whip the cream and stir it into the soup just before serving.

Prawn kromeskies

6 oz prawns (shelled and chopped), or packet of frozen prawns
½ pint thick béchamel sauce
4 oz button mushrooms (sliced)
½ oz butter
2 egg yolks
salt and pepper
½-¾ lb streaky bacon rashers

For fritter batter
5 oz plain flour
pinch of salt
¼ oz yeast
½ pint warm water

Deep fat bath

Method
To make the batter: sift the flour with salt, dissolve yeast in a little of the water and add to the flour with more water to make a thick cream. Leave to stand for 30 minutes.
Make the béchamel sauce and set it aside. Cook mushrooms quickly in the butter. Add them to the sauce with the prawns and the egg yolks ; season. Turn mixture on to a plate and leave until cold.
Cut away rind and rust from bacon and flatten rashers on a board with the blade of a knife. Put 2 rashers together so that they overlap slightly, place 1 dessertspoon of mixture at one end, then roll up. Heat the fat bath to 375°F.
Drop the kromeskies, one at a time, into the batter, making sure that they are completely covered before lifting out with a draining spoon and dropping into the hot fat. Leave enough room for them to expand. Fry until a deep golden-brown ; drain on absorbent paper. Serve hot.

Prawn pilaf

8 oz long grain rice
pinch of saffron
1 onion
2 oz butter
salt and pepper
1¼-1½ pints chicken stock, or
  bouillon cubes
2 tablespoons grated Parmesan
  cheese

For prawn salpicon
8 oz prawns (shelled)
1 oz butter
1 shallot (finely chopped)
8 oz tomatoes
1 teaspoon paprika pepper
1 teaspoon tomato purée
salt
pepper (ground from mill)
pinch of granulated sugar
few whole prawns (to garnish)
  — optional

*7-inch diameter border, or ring,
  mould (1¾-pint capacity)*

*After turning rice out of the ring
mould, carefully spoon the prawn
salpicon mixture into the centre*

Method

Set the oven at 375°F or Mark 5 and butter mould. Soak saffron in an egg cup of boiling water for 30 minutes.

Slice the onion finely, put into a pan with two-thirds of the butter, cover and cook slowly until soft but not coloured. Add the rice and fry for 2-3 minutes until it looks almost transparent. Then add the saffron and its liquid, seasoning and 1¼ pints of stock. Bring to the boil, stir once with a fork, then cover ; put in the oven and cook for 20-30 minutes or until rice is tender and the stock absorbed. If after 20 minutes it is not quite tender but all the stock has been absorbed, add the extra stock.

When rice is cooked remove from oven, dot the remaining butter over the top, dust with the cheese, cover and leave to absorb these for 5-10 minutes.

Meanwhile prepare the salpicon. Melt the butter in a pan, add chopped shallot, cover and cook slowly until soft. Scald, skin and quarter the tomatoes and scoop out the seeds ; rub seeds in a strainer and keep the juice. Add paprika to the shallot, cook for 1 minute, then stir in the tomato purée and juice from the seeds. Season and add a pinch of sugar. Simmer for 2-3 minutes. Add shelled prawns and tomatoes to the pan and toss well over the heat.

Stir the topping of butter and cheese into the rice with a fork and then spoon pilaf carefully into the buttered mould ; press lightly, turn on to a hot serving dish and spoon the prawn salpicon into the centre. Garnish with whole prawns if wished.

Scampi provençale

1 lb scampi
seasoned flour
1 oz butter (to sauté)
3 oz button mushrooms (sliced)
3 tomatoes (skinned, hard stalk
 and seeds removed)
5 oz long grain rice (boiled)
 — for serving

For sauce
2 shallots (finely chopped)
bouquet garni
1 wineglass white wine
1 oz butter
$\frac{1}{2}$ oz plain flour
1 clove of garlic (crushed with
 $\frac{1}{2}$ teaspoon salt)
1 teaspoon tomato purée
$\frac{1}{2}$ pint good stock

Method
Prepare the sauce. Simmer shallots with bouquet garni and wine until liquor is reduced by half, then remove bouquet garni and set sauce aside.

Melt $\frac{1}{2}$ oz butter, add flour off the heat, brown lightly, then add garlic, tomato purée and stock. Simmer for 10-15 minutes, then pour in reduced wine and cook a further 5 minutes. Draw aside and add small shavings of butter. Keep hot.

Roll scampi in seasoned flour and sauté lightly in 1 oz butter for 5-6 minutes. Lift into serving dish. Sauté the mushrooms in the pan and add to the sauce with the tomatoes, roughly chopped. Reboil for 1 minute, then spoon over scampi. Serve with rice.

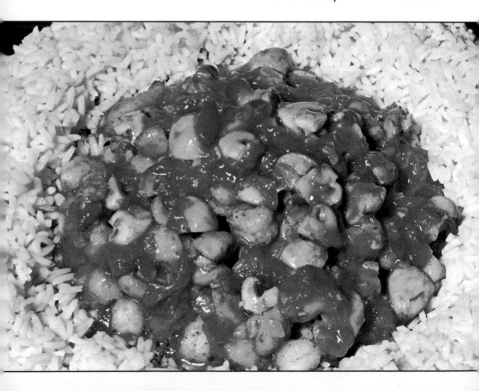

Scampi in batter

with Alabama sauce

1 lb scampi
deep fat (for frying)
fried parsley (optional)

For fritter batter
6 oz plain flour
scant $\frac{1}{4}$ oz yeast (creamed with 1
    teaspoon caster sugar)
1 tablespoon oil
$\frac{1}{2}$ pint tepid water
salt and pepper

Method
Prepare batter (see method page 16) and leave to stand for 30 minutes. Dry scampi well and heat fat bath to 375°F for oil, 380°F for fat. Stir the batter, dip in the scampi and when completely coated drop carefully into the hot fat. Fry until golden-brown and crisp. Drain well and serve very hot, garnished with fried parsley.

Alabama sauce

1 red, or green, pepper
1 clove of garlic (crushed with salt)
2-3 sticks of celery (chopped)
$\frac{1}{4}$ pint boiled dressing (see right)
$2\frac{1}{2}$ fl oz double cream
1 teaspoon horseradish cream
2-3 tablespoons tomato chutney
caster sugar
salt and pepper
dash of Tabasco sauce

Method
Split, seed and chop pepper. Blanch, refresh and drain. Stir it into dressing with the remaining ingredients. Season highly with sugar, salt and pepper to taste, and a dash of Tabasco.

This sauce should have the consistency of mayonnaise.

Boiled dressing

1 tablespoon granulated sugar
1 dessertspoon plain flour
1 teaspoon salt
1 dessertspoon made mustard
1 tablespoon water
$\frac{1}{4}$ pint each vinegar and water
    (mixed)
1 egg
$\frac{1}{2}$ oz butter
cream, or creamy milk

Method
Mix dry ingredients together, add mustard and about 1 tablespoon water. Add this mixture to vinegar and water and cook thoroughly for about 5 minutes. Beat egg, add butter, pour on the hot vinegar mixture and beat thoroughly.

When cold, dilute with a little cream or milk and mix well. This dressing keeps well, covered, in a refrigerator.

Scampi au gratin

4 oz packet of scampi
2 scallops
1 oz butter
1 glass sherry
squeeze of lemon juice
$\frac{1}{2}$ oz plain flour
$\frac{1}{4}$ pint milk
salt
pepper (ground from mill)
1 tablespoon grated Parmesan
   cheese

Prawns may be used instead of scampi for this recipe.

Method

Melt half the butter in a pan, put in the scampi and the scallops and sauté very lightly for 1-2 minutes (just enough to firm the fish on all sides). Pour on the sherry and allow it to reduce to half quantity, then add the lemon juice. Tip the fish mixture into a small gratin dish and set aside.

Melt remaining butter in the same pan, stir in the flour and blend in the milk off the heat. Season, return pan to heat and stir until sauce is boiling and it thickens, then spoon over the fish. Dust the top with the Parmesan cheese and bake in oven, pre-set at 350°F or Mark 4, or place under a hot grill for 5-8 minutes or until browned.

Scampi à la crème

1 lb scampi
1 oz butter
1 teaspoon paprika pepper
1 glass sherry
3 egg yolks
$7\frac{1}{2}$ fl oz double cream
4 tomatoes (skinned, quartered, seeds removed and the quarters cut in half)
5 oz long grain rice (boiled)
   — for serving

Method

Heat the scampi gently in the butter, add the paprika and flame with the sherry ; boil so as to reduce liquid by half.

Blend the egg yolks with the cream, strain into the pan and cook carefully until the sauce coats the back of a spoon. Add the tomatoes, season to taste, turn into a warm dish to serve. Serve with boiled rice.

Shrimps Mariette

4 oz shelled fresh, or frozen
  shrimps
round croûtes of bread (1-1½ inches
  in diameter)
salt
pinch of papper, or cayenne
  pepper, or Tabasco sauce
½ oz butter

For cheese cream
½ oz butter
½ oz plain flour
¼ pint creamy milk
1½ oz cheese (grated)
salt and pepper
English mustard

Method
Heat some oil or butter and fry
the croûtes until golden-brown,
drain and keep warm. Toss the
shrimps over heat with the
seasoning and butter and, when
this mixture is thoroughly hot,
pile it up on the croûtes. Put
these in a flameproof dish and
keep warm while preparing the
cheese cream. Proceed as if
making a white sauce ; finish
by gradually beating in the
grated cheese. Season lightly
and add mustard to taste. Spoon
this cheese cream over the
prepared croûtes and brown
well under grill. Serve very hot.

Scallops

Scallops, when alive, have their shells tightly closed, but they are usually bought ready prepared (opened and cleaned).

The easiest way to open them yourself is to put the shells into a hot oven for 4-5 minutes. The heat will cause the shells to gape. Carefully scrape away the fringe or beard which surrounds the scallop, attached to the flat shell, and the black thread (the intestine) which lies round it.

Then slip a sharp knife under the scallop to detach it and the roe from the shell. Scrub the shells thoroughly, and use for serving.

Frozen scallops are already prepared.

Scallops take only 6-7 minutes to cook and, like all shellfish, should be simmered — not boiled (which makes them tough and tasteless). They can also be baked, fried or grilled.

Scallops mornay

6 scallops
1 slice of onion
6 peppercorns
$\frac{1}{2}$ bayleaf
few parsley stalks
3-4 tablespoons water
creamed potatoes (for piping)

For mornay sauce
1 oz butter
1 oz plain flour
$\frac{1}{2}$ pint milk
liquid from scallops
2 rounded tablespoons grated
   cheese (preferably half Parmesan,
   half Gruyère)

Method
After removing from shell, wash and dry scallops and place in a pan with onion, peppercorns, herbs and water. Cover and simmer for 5-6 minutes, then drain and reserve liquid.

To prepare sauce : melt butter in a pan, remove from heat, blend in flour and then milk. Stir over gentle heat until boiling, strain on the liquid from the scallops, boil to reduce for 2-3 minutes. Remove from the heat, allow to cool, then beat in the cheese a little at a time, reserving 1 tablespoon.

Quarter the scallops and arange in buttered shells or gratin dishes. Spoon over sauce, dust with cheese and brown in a hot oven, or under the grill.

You can pipe a thick border of creamed potato round the shells before setting them on a baking sheet for browning. Fix shells in place with a little creamed potato, or wedge them with a piece of raw potato.

Coquilles St. Jacques armoricaine

5-6 good-size scallops
4-6 peppercorns
squeeze of lemon juice
1 bayleaf
1-2 tablespoons grated Cheddar,
   or Gruyère, cheese

For mirepoix
1 medium large carrot (finely
   diced)
2-3 sticks of celery (finely diced)
1 large, or 2 small, leeks (finely
   sliced)
1 oz butter
2-3 brussels sprouts (finely sliced)
2 tablespoons white wine, or water,
   or 1-2 tomatoes (scalded,
   skinned, seeds removed)

For white sauce
$\frac{1}{2}$ oz butter
$\frac{1}{2}$ oz plain flour
$7\frac{1}{2}$ fl oz creamy milk
salt and peper

*Coquilles St. Jacques armoricaine
are sprinkled with grated cheese
and quickly browned in the shells*

Method
Wash and clean the scallops
and put them into a pan. Cover
with cold water, add the peppercorns, lemon juice and bayleaf
and bring to the boil ; poach for
6-7 minutes.

Set the oven at 350°F or
Mark 4. To prepare the mirepoix : put carrot, celery and
leek in a flameproof casserole
with butter ; cover and cook on
a low heat for 3-4 minutes. Add
the sliced brussels sprouts
and the white wine (or water,
or tomatoes). Cover and put in
oven for 5-6 minutes.

Put a spoonful of the mirepoix
into each scallop shell. Drain
the scallops, slice them into
rounds and lay these on top of
the mirepoix. Prepare the white
sauce, adding any juice from the
mirepoix to it. Season the sauce
and spoon a little over the
contents of each shell, sprinkle
with the cheese and brown under
the grill or in the oven set at
450°F or Mark 8. Serve hot.

Coquilles St. Jacques Duglére

6-8 scallops (fresh or frozen)
1 shallot, or small onion (sliced)
salt
6 peppercorns
$\frac{1}{2}$ bayleaf
scant $\frac{1}{4}$ pint water
squeeze of lemon juice
2 tomatoes
1 oz butter
1 rounded tablespoon plain flour
$\frac{1}{4}$ pint creamy milk
1 teaspoon finely chopped parsley
browned breadcrumbs
little extra butter

For potato purée
1 lb potatoes
$\frac{1}{2}$ oz butter
1 tablespoon hot milk

4-6 scallop shells

Method

First make the potato purée. Peel and boil potatoes, drain and dry them, then beat to a purée (or put through a sieve) with the butter and milk.

Wash the scallops and put in a pan with the sliced shallot or onion, seasonings and bayleaf. Pour on the water, add the lemon juice and poach gently for 5 minutes.

Watchpoint Do not let the scallops boil because this toughens them.

Scald and skin the tomatoes, cut in four, remove seeds, then cut flesh in four again.

Melt the butter in a pan, remove from heat and stir in the flour. Blend in the liquid strained from the scallops. Stir over gentle heat until liquid starts to thicken, then add the milk and bring to the boil. Simmer for 2-3 minutes, taste for seasoning, then add prepared

Spooning sauce over the cooked scallops in the shell

Potato purée is piped round before browning under the grill

tomatoes and chopped parsley.
Slice or quarter the scallops and put into 4-6 buttered, deep scallop shells ; spoon over the sauce. Pipe potato purée round each shell, sprinkle lightly with brown breadcrumbs and a few tiny shavings of the extra butter.

If you prepare dish early in the day, put it in a hot oven (about 400°F or Mark 6) for 10-15 minutes to heat through. If it is freshly cooked and scallops, potato and sauce are hot, put under the grill to brown.

Baked scallops

6 large scallops
1 oz butter (melted)
salt and pepper
squeeze of lemon juice
5 tablespoons double cream
2 rounded tablespoons fresh white breadcrumbs
4 bacon rashers (to garnish) — optional

Method
Set oven at 375°F or Mark 5. Remove scallops from shells, wash and dry well. Put 1 teaspoon of melted butter in the bottom of each of 4 shells.

Quarter the scallops and arrange in the shells. Season and add a squeeze of lemon juice. Spoon over the cream, sprinkle with the breadcrumbs and add rest of melted butter.

Bake in pre-set oven for 8-10 minutes until golden-brown. The tops may be garnished with a curl of grilled bacon.

Lobster

These are among the best of shellfish and are delicious eaten cold (freshly boiled), or hot with one of the classic sauces associated with lobster. The season in Britain is from March to October, but they are available at other times of the year, though very expensive.

When raw, lobsters are a dark greenish-blue but their shells change to a brillant red when cooked. Avoid buying very large lobsters and those that are covered in barnacles — this usually indicates tough flesh. Hen lobsters are esteemed for their coral or spawn which is used to flavour and colour lobster butter for sauces and soups, while a cock lobster is prized for its fine, slightly firmer flesh. The average weight is 1-1$\frac{1}{4}$ lb and one of this size will serve two people. Smaller lobsters, averaging lb each, are especially suitable for a first course. Again, serve half per person. Choose live lobsters that feel heavy for their size, and lively. If making a hot lobster dish, it is essential to buy them alive ; in this way double cooking is avoided so that meat and sauce will be delicious and full of flavour. The process of killing a lobster is not difficult and for the lobster it is quick and painless.

To kill a lobster : choose a sharp chopping knife. Lay the lobster out flat on a wooden board, hard shell uppermost. Have the head toward your right hand and cover the tail with a cloth. Hold lobster firmly behind the head with your left hand and with the point of the knife pierce right through the little cross mark which lies on the centre of the head. The lobster is killed at once. Use this method if the flesh is to be sautéd rather than boiled.

To split a lobster : cut through the top part of the head, turn lobster round and continue to cut through the rear part of the head and down through the tail. Open out the two halves on the board and take out the dark thread (the intestine) which runs down the tail, and a small sac usually containing weed which lies in the top part of the head. These are the only parts to be thrown away. The greenish part also in the head is the liver which should be retained as it is considered a delicacy.

To dress a lobster : rinse lobster quickly in cold water, have the court bouillon (or salted water) ready on the boil. Put in the live lobster, making sure there is sufficient liquid to cover it. Cover pan, reboil and simmer gently, allowing 20 minutes for a lobster 1 lb in weight, 30 minutes for 1$\frac{1}{2}$ lb, and over that weight, 45 minutes. Draw pan aside and cool it in the liquid. Lift out and allow lobster to get quite cold. Rub shell and whiskers with a little oil before splitting.

Lobster parisienne

To dress a lobster : split lobster in two, remove sac and intestine, and twist off the big claws. Crack these and carefully lift out the meat, removing the piece of membrane which lies down the middle of the claw. Twist (or snip off with the scissors) the small claws, being careful to keep the creamy part in the head. Using the handle of a wooden spoon, roll the small claws with this to extract the meat, then fit one into another to form a circle. This makes a good base to set the half shells on for serving. With the point of a small knife lift out the tail meat, cut diagonally into thick slices or scallops and replace them, rounded side up, in the opposite half shell. Arrange the claw meat on the head shells, set the lobster on the claw circle in the serving dish, garnish with watercress and serve mayonnaise separately.

Watchpoint If time is short omit the rolling out of the small claws, they can be used instead for garnish.

2 live lobsters ($1\frac{1}{4}$-$1\frac{1}{2}$ lb each)
court bouillon
$\frac{1}{2}$ pint mayonnaise
handful of herbs (eg. parsley, tarragon, mint and watercress stalks), cooked and sieved
3 tablespoons each carrots, turnips, peas and French beans (cooked and diced)
watercress (for garnish)

Method

Cook the lobsters in the court bouillon for 30-35 minutes and leave to cool.

Flavour and colour the mayonnaise with the herb purée, mix about half of this mixture with the vegetables. Split the lobsters and remove, the meat from the shells. Fill the shells with the vegetable salad, arrange the lobster meat on top and spoon over the remaining mayonnaise mixture. Garnish dish with watercress.

Court bouillon for shellfish

Slice 2 medium-size onions and a carrot, soften them slowly in $\frac{1}{2}$ oz butter, using a pan large enough to hold the shellfish. Add the juice of $\frac{1}{2}$ lemon, a large bouquet garni, 6 peppercorns, 2 pints water, $\frac{1}{4}$ pint white wine and 1 teaspoon salt. Simmer together for 15-20 minutes.

Lobster Cordon Bleu

2 live lobsters (about 1 lb each)
court bouillon (see page 119), or
    salted water
6 oz long grain rice
1 teaspoon paprika pepper
3-4 tablespoons French dressing
salt and pepper
½ pint thick mayonnaise
2 tablespoons tomato juice cock-
    tail, or 1 cap of pimiento with 1
    tablespoon tomato juice
good dash of Tabasco sauce
squeeze of lemon juice

To garnish
watercress and / or lettuce
    hearts

Method

Cook live lobsters in court
bouillon or salted water. When
cool, split and dress them.
Arrange on a serving dish.
Garnish with watercress and / or
lettuce.

Boil the rice until tender
(about 12 minutes), drain and
dry. Add paprika to French
dressing and fork into the rice
with plenty of seasoning.

Combine the rest of the
ingredients with mayonnaise,
sieving the pimiento if this is
used. Serve the rice and the
mayonnaise mixture separately.

Mussels

These are small shellfish found
round the shores of Britain,
Holland and France. They
live on rocks and sandbanks
and, like all shellfish, they should
be eaten as fresh as possible.

They are sold by quart measure rather than weight, and
must be tightly closed before
cooking. Examine them carefully during the first thorough
rinsing in cold water, and
sharply tap any that are not
tightly closed with the handle of
a knife. If they do not respond
by closing, discard them.

Scrub the mussels well with
a small stiff brush and pull or
scrape away any small pieces of
weed from the sides. Rinse
under a running tap, then soak
them in a bowl of fresh water ;
do not tip this water off the
mussels as this might leave sand
still in them, but lift them into
another bowl or colander and
wash again. When thoroughly
clean, lift them out and put into
a large pan for cooking.

If mussels have to be kept
overnight, store in a bowl
without water in a cool place
and cover them with a heavy
damp cloth.

If storing mussels for a day
or two, cover them with cold
sea-water (if available) after
washing and add a good tablespoon of oatmeal. This will feed
them and keep them plump.

Some people eat the beard —
the slightly gristly ring round
the mussel — but this can be
pulled away with a fork, knife
or finger before serving. As it
is a lengthy process to take off
both top shell and beard, it is
really best left to each individual at the table.

Scrub the mussels well with a stiff brush after first rinse

Scrape off any weed left clinging to the sides of shells

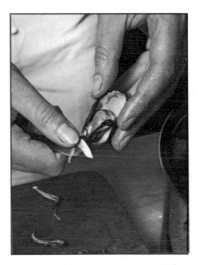

Lift (do not tip) mussels into colander so that sand from soaking water is left behind

Remove the mussels' beards before serving, or leave this to each individual at table

Italian mussel soup

1 quart mussels
4 tablespoons salad oil
1 clove of garlic (finely chopped)
1 medium-size onion (sliced)
1 medium-size can tomatoes
   (15 oz)
salt and pepper
1¼ pints stock, or water
2 wineglasses white wine
   bouquet garni (containing 2 sticks
   of celery and a strip of lemon
   rind)
2 rounded tablespoons fresh white
   breadcrumbs
1 tablespoon chopped parsley

Method

Heat the oil, add the garlic and onion and cook gently until they are golden-brown. Tip in the tomatoes and bruise well with a wooden spoon ; season lightly, pour on the stock (or water) and bring to the boil. Simmer for 15-20 minutes until reduced and pulpy.

Meanwhile scrub and wash the mussels and put them in a pan with the wine and bouquet garni. Cook over a steady heat until the mussel shells open, then remove from the heat. Strain off the liquor through muslin and add it to the soup with the breadcrumbs and simmer for 5 minutes. Shell the mussels, discarding the beards, and add them to the soup. Simmer for 5 minutes. Add the parsley and serve.

Seafood pilaf

2 pints mussels
1 wineglass white wine
¾ pint water
bouquet garni (containing
   1 stick of celery)
6 peppercorns
4 oz mushrooms
4 oz prawns, or shrimps (shelled)
1½ oz butter
pinch of ground mace
½ lb scampi

For pilaf
8 oz long grain rice
2 oz butter
1 medium-size onion (finely sliced)
1 pint chicken stock
salt and pepper

Method

Wash the mussels well, scrub them and remove any weed. Place in a large pan with the wine, water, bouquet garni, and peppercorns. Cover the pan, bring it slowly to the boil, then shake over the heat for 5 minutes. Remove mussels from shells and keep on one side.

Watchpoint Tip the liquid from the pan through a strainer lined with a piece of muslin (or even a coffee filter paper). This is to keep back any sand in the mussel liquor. Mix strained liquor with the chicken stock for the pilaf.

Set oven at 375°F or Mark 5.

To prepare the pilaf : melt two-thirds of the butter in a flameproof casserole, add the onion and cook slowly until it is soft but not coloured. Add the rice, sauté for 2-3 minutes, then add 1¼ pints of the mixed stock and mussel liquor and bring it to the boil. Taste before adding seasoning as the mussel liquor is sometimes salty enough. Place the casserole, covered, in the pre-set oven for about 20 minutes, adding extra stock, if necessary, after 15 minutes.

Meanwhile wash and trim the mushrooms and sauté quickly in 1 oz butter for 1 minute only. Add the prawns (or shrimps) and a tiny pinch of ground mace to the mushrooms and toss together for a further minute. Put the scampi in the same pan, dot with remaining $\frac{1}{2}$ oz butter, cover the pan and keep warm at the side of the stove until wanted.

When the rice for the pilaf is tender, stir in the remaining butter with a fork, then add the mussels and other shellfish.

Nova Scotia seafood platter

4 oz Nova Scotia salmon
(smoked salmon)
$\frac{1}{2}$ lb Alaskan king crab (white
crab meat)
12 jumbo shrimps, or Mediterranean
prawns, or 6 oz frozen prawns
1 packet (2 fillets) marinated
herrings (sliced on the slant)
1 small head of celery
2-3 carrots
1 Webb's, or Iceberg, lettuce
1 sweet pickled cucumber
bunch of spring onions
6 black olives
6 green olives (stuffed with
pimiento or anchovy)
$\frac{1}{4}$ pint mayonnaise
French mustard
1 carton (5 fl oz) soured cream
2-3 tablespoons tomato ketchup
dash of Tabasco sauce
1 teaspoon grated horseradish, or 2
teaspoons horseradish cream
$\frac{1}{2}$ green pepper (finely chopped)
2 tablespoons finely chopped celery

For hors d'oeuvre, guests choose from the selection of fish, accompaniments and sauces.

Method
Wash and trim the celery and carrots and cut both into even-size sticks about the length of your little finger and half as thick. Wash and dry the lettuce. Slice the pickled cucumber and prepare spring onions.

Place the crisp lettuce leaves on a large platter and arrange the fish in groups on them. Garnish with the celery and carrot sticks, cucumber, spring onions and olives.

Mix the mayonnaise with mustard to taste, and serve in a small bowl for dunking. Put the soured cream in a second small bowl. Mix the tomato ketchup with all the remaining ingredients (this sauce should be fairly hot with Tabasco and horseradish) and serve in the same way as the mustard mayonnaise.

Shellfish chowder

$\frac{1}{2}$ lb scallops
14 oz lobster meat (frozen, or
canned)
2 oz butter
$1\frac{1}{2}$ oz plain flour
$1\frac{1}{4}$ pints milk
salt and pepper
1 glass sherry
Tabasco sauce (to taste)

Method
Melt the butter in a pan, stir in the flour off the heat and blend in 1 pint of milk. Return to heat and stir well until boiling. Boil gently for 1-2 minutes and season. Wash and dry the scallops, dice and add to the sauce ; simmer for 10-15 minutes. Then add lobster meat and remaining milk ; heat gently. Taste for seasoning, add sherry and Tabasco sauce and allow to blend. Reheat gently and serve at once.

Gratin of seafood

1¼ lb cod fillet, or 4 frozen cod
   steaks
juice of ½ lemon
2 oz button mushrooms
4 oz prawns (shelled)
½ pint milk
slice of onion
6 peppercorns
blade of mace
1 oz butter
1 oz plain flour
salt and pepper
1 tablespoon Parmesan cheese
   (grated)

4 individual gratin dishes

Method

Set the oven at 350°F or Mark 4. If using fresh cod, discard the skin and cut fillets into fine strips. Grease 4 individual ovenproof gratin dishes (preferably with butter), put in fish and sprinkle with lemon juice. If using frozen cod, thaw, place in gratin dishes and sprinkle with lemon juice.

Wash mushrooms quickly in salted water, trim away stalks and then cut in fine slices. Sprinkle mushrooms and prawns on to the fish strips.

Put milk in a pan with the onion, peppercorns and mace, warm and remove from heat. Cover pan and leave to infuse until milk is well flavoured (at least 15 minutes). Strain the milk.

Melt butter in a saucepan, remove pan from heat and blend in flour and flavoured milk. Season, stir over gentle heat until boiling, then simmer for 1 minute. Adjust the seasoning.

Spoon sauce over the fish, sprinkle with Parmesan cheese, bake for 20-25 minutes in pre-set oven until golden-brown.

Seafood cocktail

8 oz frozen prawns, or scampi
1-2 tablespoons water with squeeze
   of lemon juice (for scampi)
   — optional
1 medium-size jar of mussels
1 small can crab claw meat
1 small can tunny fish
1 head of celery
1 small lettuce
French dressing

Prawns can, of course, be used alone for this type of cocktail.

Method
Open and drain mussels, rinse if preserved in brine. If using scampi, poach in oven with 1-2 tablespoons water with a squeeze of lemon juice. Cool in the liquid. For prawns, thaw out overnight in the refrigerator. Divide crab meat into 4-6 pieces, and tunny fish into large flakes.

Cut celery into short match-shaped pieces. Soak in iced water for 30 minutes. Wash lettuce well, tear in small pieces.

Make French dressing and season very well. Turn fish into a bowl, drain and dry celery and add to fish. Mix with enough dressing to coat mixture well. Pile into goblets with the lettuce for serving.

Seafood cocktail, an attractive and appetising starter for a dinner party

Vinaigrette of seafood

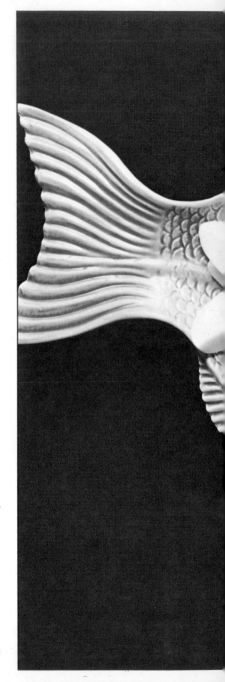

1 quart fresh mussels (cooked and removed from their shells), or canned, or bottled, mussels
6 oz prawns (shelled)
6 oz crab meat (fresh, or frozen, or canned) — flaked
2-3 beetroots (cooked)
4 new potatoes (cooked)
1 dessert apple
1 dill cucumber (sliced)
1 teacup peas (cooked)
4-5 tablespoons olive oil
2 tablespoons white wine vinegar
1 clove of garlic (crushed with pinch of salt)
sugar (to taste)
black pepper (ground from mill)
½ pint mayonnaise

For garnish
½ pint prawns (shelled)
lettuce hearts, or ½ cucumber (sliced)
few sprigs of watercress
4 hard-boiled eggs (quartered)

Method

Place all the fish in a large bowl. Dice the beetroot, potatoes and apple and add to the fish with the dill cucumber and peas. Work in the oil and vinegar with 2 forks and season well with the garlic and sugar. Add a little black pepper and leave mixture to mellow for 20 minutes, then mix in enough mayonnaise to bind fish and vegetables together.

Pile vinaigrette in serving dish, coat it with remaining mayonnaise ; arrange garnish around.

Vinaigrette of seafood makes a very attractive dish

Seafood flan

½-¾ lb mixed shellfish (eg.
   prawns, scallops and mussels)
¼ lb button mushrooms (sliced)
½ oz butter
1 green pepper (blanched, seeds
   and core removed, and shredded)
6 oz quantity of flaky, or puff, pastry
1 egg (beaten)

For sauce
1 shallot (chopped)
1 oz butter
1 teaspoon curry powder
1 oz plain flour
scant ¾ pint milk
salt and pepper
2 tablespoons double cream

*Deep 8-inch diameter pie plate, or
   9-inch long pie dish*

Method

First prepare filling: sauté mushrooms in ½ oz butter. Prepare the shellfish; if using scallops or mussels have them previously cooked and the prawns shelled or carefully thawed out. Mix shellfish with the green pepper and mushrooms.

To prepare sauce: soften shallot in the butter, add curry powder and, after 1 minute, stir in the flour off the heat. Pour on milk, blend, then return pan to heat and stir until boiling. Season and finish with the cream. Pour sauce over the shellfish, mix together carefully and turn into the pie plate or dish. Set oven at 400°F or Mark 6.

When mixture is cold, roll out pastry to a thickness of ¼-½ inch, cover pie with the pastry; decorate it and brush lightly with beaten egg. Bake in pre-set oven for 25-30 minutes or until well browned, then serve.

Appendix

Notes and basic recipes

Almonds

Buy them with their skins on. This way they retain their oil better. Blanching to remove the skins gives extra juiciness.

To blanch : pour boiling water over the shelled nuts, cover the pan and leave until cool. Then the skins can be easily removed (test one with finger and thumb). Drain, rinse in cold water, press skins off with fingers. Rinse, dry thoroughly.

To shred almonds : first blanch, skin, split in two and cut each half lenthways in fine pieces. These can then be used as they are or browned quickly in the oven, with or without a sprinking of caster sugar.

Aspic jelly

$2\frac{1}{2}$ fl oz sherry
$2\frac{1}{2}$ fl oz white wine
2 oz gelatine
$1\frac{3}{4}$ pints cold stock
1 teaspoon white wine vinegar
2 egg whites

Method

Add wines to gelatine and set aside. Pour cold stock into scalded pan, add vinegar. Whisk egg whites to a froth, add them to the pan, set over moderate heat and whisk backwards and downwards until the stock is hot. Then add gelatine, which by now will have absorbed the wine, and continue whisking steadily until boiling point has been reached.

Stop whisking and allow liquid to rise to the top of the pan ; turn off heat or draw pan aside and leave to settle for about 5 minutes, then bring it again to the boil, draw pan aside once more and leave liquid to settle. At this point the liquid should look clear ; if not, repeat the boiling-up process.

Filter the jelly through a cloth or jelly bag.

The aspic should be allowed to cool before use.

The stock for aspic jelly may be white (chicken or veal), brown (beef) or fish, according to the dish being made.

Breadcrumbs

To make crumbs : take a large loaf (the best type to use is a sandwich loaf) at least two days old. Cut off the crust and keep to one side. Break up bread into crumbs either by rubbing through a wire sieve or a Mouli sieve, or by working in an electric blender.

To make dried crumbs : spread crumbs on a sheet of paper laid on a baking tin and cover with another sheet of paper to keep off any dust. Leave to dry in a warm temperature — the plate rack, or warming drawer, or the top of the oven, or even the airing cupboard, is ideal. The crumbs may take a day or two to dry thoroughly, and they must be crisp before storing in a jar. To make them uniformly fine, sift them through a wire bowl strainer.

To make browned crumbs : bake the crusts in a slow oven until golden-brown, then crush or grind through a mincer. Sift and store as for dried white crumbs. These browned ones are known as raspings and are used for any dish that is coated with a sauce and browned in the oven.

Butter, savoury

When these mixtures are made, either serve hot or pat into balls with butter 'hands' (wooden shaping boards), or spread $\frac{1}{4}$-$\frac{1}{2}$ inch thick on greaseproof paper and chill. Then cut into small round or square pats before using. The quantities given are enough for 4 people.

Anchovy butter

2 oz unsalted butter
4 anchovy fillets (soaked in milk to remove excess salt)
black pepper (ground from mill)
anchovy essence

Method
Soften the butter on a plate with a palette knife and then crush or pound the anchovies, adding these to the butter with ground pepper and enough essence to strengthen the flavour and give a delicate pink colour.
Serve chilled, in pats.

Maître d'hôtel butter

2 oz unsalted butter
1 dessertspoon chopped parsley
few drops of lemon juice
salt and pepper

Method
Soften the butter on a plate with a palette knife, then add parsley, lemon juice and seasoning to taste.
Serve chilled, in pats.

Noisette butter

1-2 oz butter
juice of ½ lemon

Method
Melt the butter in a pan and, when brown, add the lemon juice. Use while still foaming.

Orange butter

2 oz unsalted butter
grated rind of ½ an orange and 1 teaspoon juice
1 teaspoon tomato purée
salt and pepper

Method
Soften the butter on a plate with a palette knife, and then add other ingredients, seasoning to taste.
Serve chilled, in pats.

Parsley butter

½ oz butter
1 teaspoon parsley (chopped)
dash of Worcestershire sauce, or squeeze of lemon juice

Method
Melt the butter in a pan and, when light and brown, add the chopped parsley and Worcestershire sauce or lemon juice. Blend together and then pour sauce over the fish.

Chutney, garlic, mustard or tomato butters

Other savoury butters are made in the same way using 2 oz unsalted butter with either pounded chutney, crushed garlic, 1 dessertspoon French mustard, or tomato purée.
Serve chilled, in pats.

French dressing

Mix 1 tablespoon wine, or tarragon, vinegar with ½ teaspoon each of salt and freshly ground black pepper. Add 3 tablespoons of salad oil.

When dressing thickens, taste for correct seasoning ; if it is sharp yet oily, add more salt. Quantities should be in the ratio of 1 part vinegar to 2 parts oil.

For **vinaigrette dressing,** add freshly chopped herbs of choice.

Gelatine

As gelatine setting strength varies according to brand, it is essentiel to follow instructions given on the pack. For instance, Davis gelatine recommend 1 oz to set 2 pints of liquid.

133

Mayonnaise
2 egg yolks
salt and pepper
dry mustard
$\frac{3}{4}$ cup of salad oil
2 tablespoons wine vinegar

This recipe will make $\frac{1}{2}$ pint.

Method
Work egg yolks and seasonings with a small whisk or wooden spoon in a bowl until thick ; then start adding the oil drop by drop. When 2 table-spoons of oil have been added this mixture will be very thick. Now care-fully stir in 1 teaspoon vinegar.

The remaining oil can then be added a little more quickly, either 1 tablespoon at a time and beaten thoroughly between each addition until it is absorbed, or in a thin steady stream if you are using an electric beater.

When all the oil has been absor-bed, add remaining vinegar to taste, and extra salt and pepper as neces-sary.

To thin and lighten mayonnaise add a little hot water. For a coating consistency, thin with a little cream or milk.

Eggs should not come straight from the refrigerator. If oil is cloudy or chilled, it can be slightly warmed which will lessen the chances of eggs curdling. Put oil bottle in a pan of hot water for a short time.

Watchpoint Great care must be taken to prevent mayonnaise cur-dling. Add oil drop by drop at first and then continue adding it very slowly.

If mayonnaise curdles, start with a fresh yolk in another bowl and work well with seasoning, then add the curdled mixture to it very slowly and carefully. When curdled minture is completely incorporated. more oil can be added if the mix-ture is too thin.

Parsley, fried
Choose 6-7 sprays of fresh parsley. Wash and dry well. Once fish is fried and taken out, put the indivi-dual parsley sprigs into the basket.

To avoid fat spluttering, turn off heat, wait until any blue haze has disappeared, then gently lower basket into the fat and fry for 1-2 minutes when parsley will be crisp and bright green. Drain on absorbent paper.

Pastry

Flaky pastry
8 oz plain flour
pinch of salt
3 oz butter
3 oz lard
$\frac{1}{4}$ pint ice-cold water

Method
Sift the flour with salt into a bowl. Divide the fats into four portions (two of butter, two of lard) ; rub one portion — either lard or butter — into the flour and mix to a firm dough with cold water. The amount of water varies with different flour but an average quantity for 8 oz flour is 4-5 fl oz (about $\frac{1}{4}$ pint or 8-10 tablespoons) ; the finer the flour the more water it will absorb.

Knead the dough lightly until smooth, then roll out to an oblong. Put a second portion of fat (not the same kind as the first portion rubbed in) in small pieces on to two-thirds of the dough. Fold in three, half turn the dough to bring the open edge towards you and roll out again to an oblong. Put on a third portion of fat in pieces, fold dough in three, wrap in a cloth or polythene bag and leave in a cool place for 15 minutes.

Roll out dough again, put on the remaining fat in pieces, fold and roll as before. If pastry looks at all streaky, give one more turn and roll again.

Puff pastry

8 oz plain flour
pinch of salt
8 oz butter
1 teaspoon lemon juice
scant $\frac{1}{4}$ pint water (ice cold)

Method
Sift flour and salt into a bowl. Rub in a piece of butter the size of a walnut. Add lemon juice to water, make a well in centre of flour and pour in about two-thirds of the liquid. Mix with a palette, or round-bladed, knife. When the dough is beginning to form, add remaining water.

Turn out the dough on to a marble slab, a laminated-plastic work top, or a board, dusted with flour. Knead dough for 2-3 minutes, then roll out to a square about $\frac{1}{2}$-$\frac{3}{4}$ inch thick.

Beat butter, if necessary, to make it pliable and place in centre of dough. Fold this up over butter to enclose it completely (sides and ends over centre like a parcel). Wrap in a cloth or piece of grease-proof paper and put in the refrigerator for 10-15 minutes.

Flour slab or work top, put on dough, the join facing upwards, and bring rolling pin down on to dough 3-4 times to flatten it slightly.

Now roll out to a rectangle about $\frac{1}{2}$-$\frac{3}{4}$ inch thick. Fold into three, ends to middle, as accurately as possible, if necessary pulling the ends to keep them rectangular. Seal the edges with your hand or rolling pin and turn pastry half round to bring the edge towards you. Roll out again and fold in three (keep a note of the 'turns' given). Set pastry aside in refrigerator for 15 minutes.

Repeat this process, giving a total of 6 turns with a 15-minute rest after each two turns. Then leave in the refrigerator until wanted.
Watchpoint Always roll the dough away from you, keeping the pressure as even as possible.

Rich shortcrust pastry

8 oz plain flour
pinch of salt
6 oz butter
1 egg yolk
2-3 tablespoons cold water

Method
Sift the flour with a pinch of salt into a mixing bowl. Drop in the butter and cut it into the flour until the small pieces are well coated. Then rub them in with the fingertips until the mixture looks like fine breadcrumbs. Mix egg yolk with water, tip into the fat and flour and mix quickly with a palette knife to a firm dough.

Turn on to a floured board and knead lightly till smooth. If possible, chill in refrigerator (wrapped in greaseproof paper, a polythene bag or foil) for 30 minutes before using.

Shortcrust pastry

8 oz plain flour
pinch of salt
4-6 oz butter, margarine, lard or shortening (one of the commercially prepared fats), or a mixture of any two
3-4 tablespoons cold water

Method
Sift the flour with a pinch of salt into a mixing bowl. Cut the fat into the flour with a round-bladed knife and, as soon as the pieces are well coated with flour, rub in with the fingertips until the mixture looks like fine breadcrumbs.

Make a well in the centre, add the water (reserving about 1 tablespoon) and mix quickly with a knife. Press together with the fingers, adding the extra water, if necessary, to give a firm dough.

Turn on to a floured board, knead pastry lightly until smooth. Chill in refrigerator (wrapped in greaseproof paper, a polythene bag, or foil) for 30 minutes before using.

Baking blind

A flan case should sometimes be pre-cooked before filling. Once the flan ring is lined with pastry, chill for about 30 minutes to ensure the dough is well set.

Now line the pastry with crumpled greaseproof paper, pressing it well into the dough at the bottom edge and sides.

Three-parts fill the flan with uncooked rice or beans (to hold the shape) and put into the oven to bake. An 8-inch diameter flan ring holding a 6-8 oz quantity of pastry should cook for about 26 minutes in an oven at 400°F or Mark 6.

After about 20 minutes of the cooking time take flan out of the oven and carefully remove the paper and rice, or beans. (Rice, or beans, may be used many times over for baking blind.) Replace the flan in the oven to complete cooking. The ring itself can either be taken off with the paper and rice, or removed after cooking. Once cooked, slide the flan on to a wire rack and then leave to cool.

Potatoes

Baked (jacket) potatoes
1 large potato per person
salt
pat of butter per person
parsley (optional)

Method
Well scrub large, even-size potatoes and roll them in salt. Bake for $1\frac{1}{2}$ hours (or until they give when pressed) in an oven at 375°F or Mark 4. Make crosscuts on top of each potato and squeeze to enlarge cuts. Put a pat of butter and sprig of parsley in centre ; serve at once.

Chip potatoes (French fried)

$1\frac{1}{2}$ lb even-size potatoes
(weighed when peeled)
deep fat, or at least 1-inch depth of fat in frying pan

Method
Prepare potatoes 1 hour before needed. Square off ends and sides of potatoes, cut in $\frac{1}{2}$-inch thick slices, then into thick fingers. Soak in cold water for 30 minutes, then drain. Wrap in absorbent paper or cloth and leave for 20-30 minutes. Heat fat, dip in empty basket ; when fat reaches 350°F gently lower potatoes in basket into fat. If you do not have a thermometer, drop in a finger of potato ; if this rises to surface at once and fat starts to bubble gently, fat is ready. Fry gently until potatoes are just soft but not coloured. Lift out and drain, still in basket, on a plate. Chips can be left like this for a little while before the final frying. Reheat fat to 360-375°F ; carefully lower in basket, fry chips to a deep golden-brown. Drain well on absorbent paper, turn into a hot dish for serving and sprinkle with salt. Potatoes double-fried in this way are crisply tender on the outside and evenly browned. When cooking fish and chips, fry potatoes first so that there is no chance of crumb coating from fish spoiling the fat for the potatoes.

Creamed potatoes (for piping)
Boil peeled potatoes, drain and dry well. Mash or put through a Mouli sieve.

Gradually beat in boiling milk ($\frac{1}{2}$ pint to every $1\frac{1}{2}$ lb potatoes) with about 1 oz butter and season to taste. This can be kept hot for up to 30 minutes by covering the levelled surface in the pan with 2-3 tablespoons of hot milk and the lid. Beat up before piping (use a vegetable rose pipe).

'Fish' potatoes

These are shaped from old potatoes and get their name because they so frequently accompany fish dishes. Choose medium-size potatoes, peel and quarter them lengthways. Pare away sharp edges with a peeler and shape into ovals. Boil in a pan of salted water about 7 minutes, drain and return to pan. Cover with some foil or muslin and the pan lid. Complete cooking on a low heat until tender (about 4-5 minutes).

This treatment prevents potatoes from breaking and makes them dry and floury.

Rice (boiled)

There are almost as many ways of cooking rice as there are cooks, so if you have your own well-tried method stick to it, but if you have problems, the following method is foolproof.

Allow 2 oz of washed rice per person.

Shower the rice into a large pan of boiling, salted water, at least 3 quarts for 8 oz, and add a slice of lemon for flavour. Stir with a fork to prevent sticking and boil steadily for about 12 minutes until tender. Rice very quickly overcooks so watch its cooking time carefully.

To stop rice cooking, tip it quickly into a colander and drain, or pour $\frac{1}{2}$ cup of cold water into the pan and drain in a colander.

Then pour over a jug of hot water to wash away remaining starch, making several holes through the rice (with the handle of a wooden spoon) to help it drain more quickly. Turn on to a large meat dish and leave in a warm place to dry.

Turn rice from time to time with a fork.

For easy reheating, spoon rice into a well buttered, shallow ovenproof dish which should be small enough for the rice to fill it amply. Place a sheet of well-buttered paper over the top. The rice can then be reheated and served in this dish. Allow 30 minutes in the oven at 350°F or Mark 4.

Sauces

Béchamel sauce

$\frac{1}{2}$ **pint milk**
1 slice of onion
1 small bayleaf
6 peppercorns
1 blade of mace

For roux
$\frac{3}{4}$ **oz butter**
1 rounded tablespoon plain flour
salt and pepper

Method
Pour milk into a saucepan, add the flavourings, cover pan and infuse on gentle heat for 5-7 minutes. Strain milk and set it aside. Rinse and wipe out the pan and melt the butter in it. Remove pan from heat and stir in the flour to make a soft, semi-liquid roux.

Pour on half the milk and blend until smooth, using a wooden spoon. Add rest of milk and season lightly. Return pan to heat and stir until boiling. Boil for no longer than 2 minutes.

Hollandaise sauce

4 tablespoons white wine vinegar
6 peppercorns
1 blade of mace
1 slice of onion
1 small bayleaf
3 egg yolks
5 oz unsalted butter
salt and pepper
1-2 tablespoons single cream, or milk
squeeze of lemon juice (optional)

137

Method

Put the vinegar into a small pan with the spices, onion and bayleaf. Boil this until reduced to a scant tablespoon, then set aside.

Cream egg yolks in a bowl with a good nut of butter and a pinch of salt. Strain on the vinegar mixture, set the bowl on a pan of boiling water, turn off heat and add remaining butter in small pieces, stirring vigorously all the time.

Watchpoint When adding butter, it should be slightly soft, not straight from refrigerator.

When all the butter has been added and the sauce is thick, taste for seasoning and add the cream or milk and lemon juice. The sauce should be pleasantly sharp yet bland, and should have consistency of thick cream.

Mornay (cheese) sauce

Make ½ pint white or béchamel sauce, remove from heat and gradually stir in 2-3 rounded tablespoons grated cheese. When well mixed, add ½ teaspoon made mustard. Reheat but do not boil.

Mustard sauce

Make ½ pint velouté sauce and mix 1 teaspoon made mustard with 1 tablespoon of the sauce, then stir this mixture into the sauce.

Parsley sauce

1 large handful of fresh parsley (picked from stalks)
½ pint velouté sauce

Method

Make velouté sauce. Wash parsley sprigs, boil for 7 minutes in pan of salted water ; drain, press out moisture, then rub through a wire strainer. Beat into hot velouté sauce.

Or add cooked drained parsley to half the sauce without sieving and work in an electric blender.

Suprême sauce

1 oz butter
¾ oz plain flour
½ pint strong fish stock

For liaison
2-3 egg yolks
¼ pint single cream

Method

Make up as for velouté sauce. Then work the egg yolks and cream together and mix with 1 tablespoon of the hot sauce. Add this liaison very slowly to the sauce, then reheat carefully.

Tartare sauce

2 eggs (hard-boiled)
1 egg yolk (raw)
salt and pepper
½ pint oil
1 tablespoon vinegar
1 teaspoon chopped parsley
1 teaspoon snipped chives
1 teaspoon chopped capers, or gherkins

Method

Cut the hard-boiled eggs in half, remove the yolks and rub them through a strainer into a bowl. Add the raw yolk and seasoning ; work well together. Add the oil drop by drop, as for a mayonnaise, and dilute with the vinegar as necessary. Finish off with the herbs and capers. If wished, add the shredded white of one of the hard-boiled eggs.

Tomato sauce

1 lb tomatoes, or 1 can (15 oz)
1 oz butter
1 rounded dessertspoon plain flour
½ pint stock, or water
bouquet garni
salt and pepper
pinch of sugar
1 teaspoon tomato purée (optional)

Method

Melt the butter in a pan, stir in the flour. Draw pan off the heat, blend in the stock or water and stir until boiling.

Cut tomatoes in half, squeeze out the seeds and strain the juice from them. Add tomatoes, juice and bouquet garni to the pan. Season to taste and add sugar ; add tomato purée to strengthen flavour if necessary. Cover pan and cook gently for 25-35 minutes until tomatoes are pulpy. Remove bouquet garni and pour sauce through a strainer, pressing it well to extract the juice. Return it to the rinsed-out pan, adjust seasoning and boil gently for about 5 minutes or until it is the right consistency.

Watchpoint The appearance is improved by stirring in $\frac{1}{2}$ oz butter just before serving. This will give the sauce a good gloss.

Velouté sauce

$\frac{3}{4}$ **oz butter**
1 rounded tablespoon plain flour
$\frac{1}{3}$-$\frac{1}{2}$ **pint stock**
2$\frac{1}{2}$ fl oz top of milk
salt and pepper
squeeze of lemon juice

For liaison (optional)
1 egg yolk (lightly beaten)
2 tablespoons cream

Method

Melt butter in a saucepan, stir in flour and cook for about 5 seconds. When roux is colour of pale straw, draw pan aside and cool slightly before pouring on stock.

Blend, return to heat and stir until thick. Add top of milk, season and bring to boil. Cook for 4-5 minutes when sauce should be a syrupy consistency. If using a liaison prepare by mixing egg yolk and cream together and then stir into sauce. Add lemon juice.

Remove pan from heat.

Watchpoint Be careful not to let sauce boil after liaison has been added, otherwise the mixture will curdle.

White sauce

$\frac{3}{4}$ **oz butter**
1 rounded tablespoon plain flour
$\frac{1}{2}$ **pint milk**
salt and pepper

Method

Melt the butter in a pan, remove from heat and stir in the flour. Blend in half the milk, then stir in the rest. Stir over moderate heat until boiling, then boil gently for 1-2 minutes. Season to taste.

Stocks

Chicken stock

This should ideally be made from the giblets (neck, gizzard, heart and feet, if available), but never the liver which imparts a bitter flavour. This is better kept for making pâté, or sautéd and used as a savoury. Dry fry the giblets with an onion, washed but not peeled, and cut in half. To dry fry, use a thick pan with a lid, with barely enough fat to cover the bottom. Allow the pan to get very hot before putting in the giblets and onion, cook on full heat until lightly coloured. Remove pan from heat before covering with 2 pints of cold water. Add a large pinch of salt, a few peppercorns and a bouquet garni (bayleaf, thyme, parsley) and simmer gently for 1-2 hours.

Fish stock
1 medium-size onion
1½ lb sole bones
½ oz butter
6 white peppercorns
small bouquet garni
juice of ½ lemon
salt
2 pints water
Method
Slice the onion, blanch and refresh.
Wash the sole bones well and drain
them. Melt the butter in a large pan
and put in the prepared onion, sole
bones, peppercorns, bouquet garni,
lemon juice and salt.

Cover the pan and put over very
gentle heat for 10 minutes. Add the
water, bring to the boil and skim
well. Simmer gently for 20 minutes,
then strain through a fine nylon
strainer. Leave stock to cool ; when
cold, cover and keep in refrigerator
until wanted.

Veal (white bone) stock
3 lb veal bones
2 onions (quartered)
2 carrots (quartered)
1 stick of celery (sliced)
large bouquet garni
6 peppercorns
3-4 quarts water
salt

*6-quart capacity saucepan, or small
fish kettle*

Method
Wipe bones but do not wash them
unless unavoidable. Put them in a
large pan with the water, bring
slowly to the boil, skimming from
time to time to remove fat. When
the fat has been skimmed off the
liquid, add the vegetables, bouquet
garni and seasoning.

Simmer for 4-5 hours, or until
the stock tastes strong and good.
Strain off and use the bones
again for a second boiling. Although

this second stock will not be as
strong as the first, it is good for
soups and gravies. Use the first
stock where a jellied stock is
required.

Vegetable stock
1 lb carrots
1 lb onions
½ head of celery
½ oz butter
3-4 peppercorns
1 teaspoon tomato purée
2 quarts water
salt

Method
Quarter the vegetables, and brown
them lightly in the butter in a large
pan. Add peppercorns, tomato
purée, water and salt. Bring to the
boil, cover pan and simmer for 2
hours or until the stock has a good
flavour.

Tomatoes (skinning and seeding)
To skin tomatoes, place them in a
bowl, pour boiling water over them,
count 12, then pour off the hot
water and replace it with cold. The
skin then comes off easily. Cut a
slice from the top (not stalk end)
of each tomato, reserve slices ;
hold tomato in hollow of your palm,
flick out seeds with the handle of a
teaspoon, using the bowl of the
spoon to detach the core. So much
the better if the spoon is worn and
therefore slightly sharp.

Glossary

Bain-marie (au) To cook at temperature just below boiling point in a bain-marie (a saucepan standing in a larger pan of simmering water). Used in the preparation of sauces, creams and food liable to spoil if cooked over direct heat. May be carried out in oven or on top of stove. A double saucepan gives a similar result. Sauces and other delicate dishes may be kept hot in a bain-marie at less than simmering heat.

Baste To spoon hot fat / liquid over food as it cooks in the oven.

Blanch To remove strong tastes from vegetables by bringing to the boil from cold water and draining before further cooking. Green vegetables should be put into boiling water and cooked for up to 1 minute.

Bouquet garni Traditionally a bunch of parsley, thyme, bayleaf, for flavouring stews and sauces. Other herbs can be added. Remove before serving dish.

Butter, clarified Butter which is heated gently until foaming, skimmed well and the clear yellow liquid strained off, leaving the sediment (milk solids) behind.

Butter, kneaded Butter and flour worked together to form a paste (in the proportion of 1 oz butter to $\frac{1}{2}$ oz flour). It is used to thicken liquid and is added in small pieces, usually at the end of the cooking process. When the exact quantity of liquid is unknown this is the quickest way to thicken.

Croûte Small round of bread, lightly toasted or fried. It can be spread or piled up with a savoury mixture or used as a garnish.

Croûton Small square or dice of fried bread or potato to accompany purée or cream soups.

Egg wash Egg beaten with a pinch of salt and used as a glaze for pastry.

Glaze 1. To brown under the grill or in the oven. 2. To make shiny with egg, water or milk.

Infuse To steep in liquid (not always boiling) in a warm place to draw or in the oven. 2. To make shiny flavour into the liquid.

Liaison Mixture for thickening / binding sauce / gravy / soup, eg. roux, egg yolks and cream, kneaded butter.

Mirepoix Basic preparation for flavouring braises and sauces. Diced vegetables, sweated (cooked gently for a few minutes in butter), to draw out flavour. Diced bacon and bayleaf sometimes included.

Reduce To boil a liquid fast to reduce quantity and concentrate the flavour.

Refresh To pour cold water over previously blanched and drained food. This sets vegetable colours, cleans meat / offal.

Roux Fat and flour mixture which is the basis of all flour sauces. The fat is melted and the flour stirred in off the heat before liquid is added.

Sauté To brown food in butter, or oil and butter. Sometimes cooking is completed in a 'small' sauce - ie. one made on the food in the sauté pan.

Scald 1. To plunge into boiling water for easy peeling. 2. To heat a liquid, eg. milk, to just under boiling point.

Seasoned flour Flour to which salt and pepper have been added. To 1 tablespoon of flour add a pinch of pepper, and as much salt as you can hold between your thumb and two fingers.

Slake To mix arrowroot / cornflour with water before adding to a liquid for thickening.

141

Index